к

D0942451

DATE DUE

Southern Illinois University Press
Carbondale and Edwardsville

WHO CARES?

Women, Care, and Culture

Julia T. Wood

Edited and designed by Robyn Laur Clark
Production supervised by Natalia Nadraga

97   96   95   94   4   3   2   1

Library of Congress Cataloging-in-Publication Data

Wood, Julia T.
    Who cares? women, care, and culture / Julia T. Wood.
        p.   cm.
    Includes bibliographical references (p.   ) and index.
    1. Women—Psychology.   2. Nurturing behavior.
    3. Caregivers—United States.   I. Title.
    HQ1206W893   1994
305.4—dc20   93-16226
ISBN 0-8093-1816-4   CIP
ISBN 0-8093-1948-9 pbk.

The paper used in this publication meets the minimum requirements
of American National Standard for Information Sciences—Permanence
of Paper for Printed Library Materials, ANSI Z39.48-1984. ∞

This book is dedicated to my mother,
Frances Becker Wood,
whose life was organized around caring for others,
including me.
In so many ways she made me and my life possible.
From her I learned much about caring
and just as much about the exorbitant costs
it imposes on caregivers.

FRANCES BECKER WOOD

23 February 1923–18 March 1991

Contents

Preface

Who Cares? is about what is and what can be. It is a warning about the mounting care crisis confronting us as we stand on the brink of the twenty-first century. It is an effort to understand highly personal issues of caring that come up in our individual lives. It is an inquiry into the discursive means that create and sustain attitudes toward caring and women within our culture. It is an argument for positioning care more centrally in our cultural life and enacting the structural and symbolic changes required to realize that reconfiguration. Finally, it is an invitation to participate in reforming our society and ourselves so that we are more humanly responsive and responsible.

No single study of women, care, and culture can be comprehensive, and this book is no exception. Within these broad concerns, my inquiry focuses on discursive practices that structure culture and, thus, our understandings of women and care. The institutions and practices that comprise a culture are embodied—that is, expressed and sustained—through concrete, discursive activities of individuals, families, groups, and organizations. Studying discourse in those contexts illuminates both the existing structure of our society and the sites where it might be contested. I hope that my inquiry, in conjunction with that of many others, will contribute to a heightened awareness of the growing needs for care we face and the impossibility of fulfilling them within the current organization of our society.

Who Cares? offers no solutions, no quick fixes, no easy answers to how we might meet the care crisis in our country. To do so would be at once presumptuous and naive. I do, however, try to point to paths that might be fruitful in our efforts to address the care crisis and to locations where advocacy might be most persuasive. This, of course, does not provide an immediately satisfying resolution to the dilemma I identify. And I rather think that is desirable.

In developing his own theory of drama, Brecht indicted the narrative structure of Aristotelian drama for providing a catharsis that is all too consoling to an audience. Brecht's objection was that such catharsis relieves us of our discomfort and distress about complex issues and predicaments. In so doing, argued Brecht, it undermines sustained, serious motivation, which he saw as necessary to addressing complicated human problems. That motivation to respond can arise only out of unresolved tensions, uncathected anguish. Thus, quick judgments and answers diminish inclinations toward social reform.

The crisis of care that I discuss is real, complex, and profound for us as individuals and a people. I have no wish to narcotize discomfort or to attenuate the wholly appropriate outrage at the currently inadequate ways in which caring for others takes place in the United States. It seems only natural that we feel upset, frightened, and angry. Most of all, we need to feel compelled to do something to change prevailing structural and symbolic obstacles to caring for others without imposing severe and inequitable burdens on only selected members of society. If *Who Cares?* in any small measure invigorates and directs efforts to bring about change, then my efforts will be graciously rewarded.

Any writer has readers in mind when she or he works. In writing this book, I envisioned three different kinds of readers and tried to speak to each of them. First of all, teachers and scholars whose work focuses on caring, communication, and women's roles in contemporary Western society should find this book valuable. I try to integrate studies of women and caring conducted by academics in a host of fields with insightful analyses from clinicians working with clients whose identities as women and caregivers have caused upheaval in their lives. In addition, I offer an original analysis of one key text in the public discourse about caring, and the concluding chapter includes suggestions for addressing the problems of caring in the United States in socially and politically powerful ways.

Second, I hope clinicians working with clients confronting problems in their efforts to care for others will find merit in this book. Throughout the book I draw upon theory and case reports from therapists that complement and enrich the findings of academic research on care and the difficulties that surround it. In addition, I have made a concerted effort to emphasize the caregiver and the potential costs of focusing on the needs of others. Thus, my inquiry may amplify the insights clinicians have derived from their practice and provide an enlarged perspective within which to view the situations of particular clients.

Finally, I hope this book invites the attention of women and men whose professional interests may not center on care, but whose private lives have included or currently include caring relationships. For these readers, *Who Cares?* offers a readable exploration of the kinds of care most of us at times feel we should provide and the kinds of tensions and satisfactions we typically experience in caring for others. And no matter what the background of the reader, I hope this book fuels a commitment to be part of changing our culture in ways that elevate caring to a central priority and that renovate social policies and practices so that we may care for those who need it and may be comforted in knowing that we, too, will be cared for in our times of need.

Acknowledgments

I now have the welcome opportunity to thank a number of people and institutions that have contributed to the ideas in *Who Cares?* and supported me during its gestation. I first acknowledge the University of North Carolina for awarding me a Pogue Research Leave for the fall of 1991, during which the manuscript of this book was completed. Dean Gillian T. Cell, in particular, provided material and personal assistance for this project. I also wish to thank the Department of Speech Communication, and especially my chair, William Balthrop, for furnishing research assistance. My colleagues, along with graduate and undergraduate students, have consistently stimulated and challenged me with rich, provocative, and often delightfully impertinent responses to my work. Professor Beverly Long has been exceedingly generous in both her friendship and her support of my work and personal priorities.

I am grateful to the editorial staff at SIU Press for assistance: Kenney Withers initially supported this project, and Susan Wilson supervised the book's development. Especially, I acknowledge Robyn Laur Clark, who edited the manuscript and increased the clarity of my writing.

I am indebted to the employees of Right Staff, the home health agency that mother and I came to depend on when her needs for care exceeded what my husband, sister, brother-in-law, and I were able to provide. Any misconceptions I had about the impersonalness of professional caregiving were dispelled as I saw the tenderness and attention these women gave my mother. All of the women of Right Staff developed warm, personal relationships with my mother that enhanced her life and, I hope, theirs as well. Although they had less time to get to know mother than I did, their tears at her funeral were as real as my own. So many thanks to Judy, Pat, Peggy, Frances, Shirley, and especially my "sister" Tammy, whose devotion and kindness led mother to adopt her, complete with an adoption certificate.

I am also fortunate in having had much personal support and assistance from friends during the years of work on this book. Thanks go first to Erica, Jane, Judith, Peggy, and Sarah who make up the discussion group I've belonged to for several years. These women listened sensitively and responded insightfully to my feelings and concerns about caring for mother and, more generally, to my efforts to work through a range of issues surrounding women's traditional role as caregiver. I am also indebted to Nancy, conversationalist extraordinaire, for her ongoing interest in both my life and my work, her always insightful and frequently challenging responses to my ideas about caring, and her honesty in sharing her own struggles with caring. Jerry Phillips supported me with his friendship and thoughtful daily conversations with me about both the pragmatic realities of caring and the theoretical issues entailed in this book. And I must thank Katherine Huffman, M.D., that rarest of doctors who practices medicine as both a science and an art. Kathy had the insight to recognize that caregivers need care too, and she had the compassion and medical expertise to safeguard my health.

Finally, and most importantly, I want to thank the members of my family for the many ways they contributed to this book. My brother, Charles, first taught me about caring for others. Born with brain damage, he required and still requires special attention, time, and understanding. Growing up with him as part of our family allowed me to realize the importance of compassion and also to witness the enormous costs my mother incurred in caring constantly for another person.

If any one person has taught me the most about caring it is my partner, Robbie Cox. Throughout the eighteen years of our marriage he has taught me to care by his example. Through his constancy and openness to me and the comfort he provided my mother during her time with us, he kept us aware of the rhythms of life even as we felt the relentless weight of death. He found ways of nurturing us both without ever making us dependent on him. Not only did he teach me much about caring, but he contributed to this book in important ways by extending, challenging, and affirming ideas developed in it. Finally, he has shown the good humor to be amused, rather than to feel slighted, by my preoccupation with this project. He appreciated the irony of my being so involved in writing about care that at times I wasn't very caring about him and our relationship.

This book could not have been written without the personal support and the insights of my sister Carolyn and my brother-in-law, Leigh. Throughout the years that my father and mother required care, they were there providing it with uncommon grace and generosity. Moreover, both Carolyn and Leigh offered an always-open, never-judgmental sounding board for me as I sought to grapple with the increasing responsibilities of caring for mother and we all endured the wrenching experience of watching her die. The five of us shared the responsibilities, anguish, and growth inherent in imbuing mother's final passage with love and dignity. Conversations with Leigh, Carolyn, and Robbie nourished my spirit and enlarged my understanding of the dimensions of caring as well as the dilemmas entailed in it.

Finally, I am deeply indebted to my father and mother for the many ways in which they enriched my life, not the least of which was trusting me, along with Carolyn, Leigh, and Robbie, to care for them in their final days. Both taught me much about caring, including the unique problems and opportunities possible in human relationships where substantial needs exist. Both were extraordinary teachers. And both continue to live within me and to teach me through the lasting gift of memories.

WHO CARES?

"I only hope your daughters-in-law are a tenth as good to you as you have been to me," said Mother yesterday.
"What about my sons?" I said.
She laughed. "Sons don't do like daughters."

—Diane Rubin, *Caring: A Daughter's Story*

CHAPTER 1
A Personal Introduction

Who cares? is at once an intensely personal question and a pressing social issue. In this book I hope to enlarge the understanding of both these dimensions of the concern about who does and will care. The question of who cares is personal, because each of us has to decide whether to care for others who need our help and whether there are people from whom we can expect help when we ourselves need it. Yet, caring is not only a personal issue. It is also a cultural concern. It has always been so, because the structure of our culture defines what counts as caring and who is to provide it. Further, our cultural beliefs and attitudes as embodied in our concrete activities reinforce or contest the ways we have defined caring and its importance in our social order. Historically, caring has been defined as a personal matter—one outside the purview of public concern and attention and relegated to the private sphere and thus "woman's domain." It is this, I believe, that we must change if we are to meet the care crisis that is already upon us and is growing rapidly more urgent.

This book grows out of both personal experiences and professional interests. The last decade of my life has centered on caring for both my parents through their prolonged illnesses and deaths. From these relationships and my responsibilities to protect, help, and comfort my father and mother, I learned much about what caring for others means in contemporary America. I discovered how much time, energy, and patience are required to care for others; I came to appreciate the enormous difference

1

caring can make to individuals who are ill, in pain, and facing death; and I realized some of the costs a caregiver incurs in a society that defines caring as a low priority. My personal experiences enkindled a professional interest in learning more about the nexus among caring, women, and culture.

For an even longer time—eighteen years—I have been on the faculty of the University of North Carolina, where my research and teaching focus on gender issues, interpersonal communication, and human relationships. My academic training has taught me that experience alone is seldom, if ever, sufficient for a thorough understanding. Unaugmented by broader knowledge, personal experience can lead to erroneous generalizations based on what may be distinctly atypical events in our own lives. So I seek to enhance my understanding of care by placing my own experiences within a larger framework informed by studies of caring as well as reports from others who have been involved in providing care or working with those who do.

Thus, what began as a quest to understand my own experience in caring for my parents grew into a larger inquiry, one that attempts to provide an account of the nature of caring as well as its long-standing association with the private sphere and women in Western culture. This book draws heavily on interdisciplinary research available on caring, women's roles in that process, and how the relationship between these two is discursively constituted and sustained in our culture. At the same time, from my own relationships with others I have come to appreciate in ever larger ways the extensive need for caring and the costs of it, insights that inform many of the ideas and arguments comprising this book. Since both my personal and professional positions directly influence the positions I take and the interpretations I offer within, I wish to elaborate them here in introducing the book. By disclosing my own subjective positioning, I intend to enable readers to assess how my identity and experiences are implicated in this work.

As a professor at my university, I focus on human relationships, communication, and women's roles in contemporary culture. These concerns are often related. In my classes I try to enhance students' understanding of the need for and value of caring for others—a difficult task since we live in a society that does not bestow substantial recognition and rewards on caring or those who do it. Nonetheless, my teaching emphasizes the importance of caring to our well-being as individuals and a society.

Being able and willing to care for others is essential for building strong interpersonal relationships and for creating a social fabric that allows us all to live with a modicum of comfort, security, and grace. We want to believe someone will be there for us if we cannot fully care for ourselves; we need to be there for others when they require help, nurturance, or support; most of all, we need to understand that all life is necessarily, intimately interrelated and, thus, our individual and communal lives are intertwined. How we regard people who need help and how we respond to them contribute to the overall cultural attitude that influences how others treat us when we, in our turn, need help.

To illustrate the ways in which individual actions influence larger cultural patterns that, in turn, affect us, I often share with my students the following Pakistani folktale (Silverstone & Hyman, 1989):

An ancient grandmother lived with her daughter and her grandson in a small but comfortable house not far from the village. The old woman grew frail and feeble, her eyesight became dimmer every day, and she found it hard to remember where she'd put things and what people had asked her to do. Instead of being a help around the house she became a constant trial and irritation. She broke the plates and cups, lost the knives, put out the stove, and spilled the water. One day, exasperated because the older woman had broken another precious plate, the younger one gave some money to her son and told him, "Go to the village and buy your grandmother a wooden plate. At least we will have one thing in the house she cannot break."

The boy hesitated because he knew that wooden plates were used only by peasants and servants—not by fine ladies like his grandmother—but his mother insisted, so off he went. Some time later he returned bringing not one, but two wooden plates.

"I only asked you to buy one," his mother said to him sharply. "Didn't you listen to me?"

"Yes," said the boy. "But I bought the second one so there will be one for you when you get old." (n.p.)

Caring for others and being cared for are two of the many human experiences in which we can participate and from which we can grow. In deciding whether to care for others and how to care for them we participate in the ongoing process by which a culture creates its values, values that ultimately become our own.

As important as caring is, however, it is not without hazards. In order to enhance the possibility of caring that is healthy for the one caring and the one cared for, we must understand what it involves and what potential dangers it may pose, especially for caregivers. Here we are aided by research reported by academics in speech communication, sociology, human development, psychology, philosophy, and social work as well as by insightful observations and theorizing of clinicians involved in the hands-on practice of helping people cope with the responsibilities of caring.

Two closely related conclusions can be drawn from all of this work. First, it seems that caring can be healthy and enriching when it is informed, freely chosen, and practiced within a context that recognizes and values caring and those who do it. On the other hand, existing studies also suggest that caring can be quite damaging to caregivers if they are unaware of dangers to their identities, if they have unrealistic expectations of themselves, and/or if caring occurs within contexts that fail to recognize its importance and value.

As a human being and a woman, I think caring for others is important. I cannot, in fact, remember a time when this wasn't an understood priority for me. My earliest memories of childhood are punctuated by recollections of my parents' admonishing me to "think about how your friend would feel if you did that," "you have to think of others first—put them ahead of yourself," "make time for others," "don't be selfish," and "put yourself in your sister's place, and you'll know what to do." From such injunctions I learned, as most young girls do, to think of, about, and in terms of others; I came to be more concerned with figuring out what others wanted me to give than what doing so might cost me; I learned to focus on understanding others' perspectives in order to provide them with what they needed or wanted; and I came to believe that caring for others is central to who I am and what my life should be about.

The last two decades of research on gender roles, as I will show in later chapters, indicate that my experiences were not atypical: most females are socialized to be sensitive to others and to understand that caring is an ongoing expectation of them, though not of males. If this socialization is effective, most women internalize the expectation and prompt themselves to care for others and to judge themselves as selfish if they don't give generously of their time and of themselves. This expectation comprises a double-edged issue in many women's lives. Just as empathy, nurturing, and caring can enlarge women's understandings of themselves and others and can prepare them to form relationships of extraordinary depth, so too can these qualities threaten women's ability to develop and maintain a clear sense of themselves as individuals. In the chapters that follow, I elaborate and explore the tension that arises out of the values and dangers inherent in caring as it is currently defined within our culture.

While I'd grown up being taught to care for others and had adhered to that "script" generally, it was not until 1982 that caring became a major focus of my life and my sense of who I was in terms of concrete, daily activities. That year my father, then seventy-five years old, had a stroke. While his mind was not affected, his speech and mobility were seriously impaired. My mother, ill herself, could not shoulder the full responsibility of providing the care he needed. Since I lived and worked only fifty miles from my parents' home, my father assumed that I would help mother care for him. He did not want and would not accept the help of strangers, and besides, as he explained to us, that's what family is for. I agreed and began staying with my parents on weekends.

As is usually the case with strokes, one presages others. Within eighteen months my father had two more strokes. Gradually what had begun as weekend assistance enlarged into a primary responsibility that required me to be with my parents for three to five days of every week. All the while, I maintained my duties as a faculty member and administrator on my campus, as well as my commitment to my partner and our marriage. I learned to take my work to my parents' home and to stay up late or even all night to prepare classes, grade papers, or work on research.

In the four years of my father's dying, I learned first-hand some of the consequences of caring for others. I lost over one-fourth of my body weight when I had not been overweight to start with; I suffered debilitating insomnia; and I was drained of the energy and time to be as involved with my partner as I had been during the prior nine years of our marriage. Interestingly, at the time I knew enough about women's roles and my own tendencies to understand somewhat what was happening to me, but I didn't know enough to change the course of events. I couldn't stop caring for my father and wanting to lighten the responsibilities my mother had; I refused to be distracted by, or even to recognize, my own health and needs, because I believed that caring for others was what I was supposed to do.

One of the strongest and most painful memories I have of that period is of an autumn afternoon when my father and I had a conversation about his increasing needs. It began when I suggested we should hire some nurses or aides to help out. Rejecting this proposal, my father said musingly, "It's funny, Julia. I used to wish I had sons, but now I'm glad I have daughters, because I couldn't ask a son to take this kind of time away from his own work just to take care of me."

I was stunned by his comment. In that moment I understood more clearly than all of my research and reading had ever taught me how powerful is the equation between being female and the expectation of care. I also perceived how little value is generally placed on caring for others, making it entirely consistent with societal values for my father to diminish the activity as "just" taking care of him. And I realized he was quite right on both counts. I would make time; I felt I couldn't do otherwise and still be a "good" person/woman. I had been well trained. And I knew, even while doing it, that in the eyes of many of my colleagues caring for my father was far less important and valuable than the articles and books I had published and the awards I had won in my career.

A few years after my father died, my mother's health declined to a level that made living alone impossible for her. She had always said she would not live with any of her children, because she didn't want to impose on their lives. After my father's drawn out dying process, she became even more adamant in declaring she would not disrupt our lives for her needs.

As the severity of her condition became clear, my sister, Carolyn, and I asked mother about her plans, and she said she needed to move into a nursing home. In an effort to help, I made calls and wrote letters until we were deluged with pamphlets from the various retirement centers, nursing homes, and rest homes in our state. I tried to discuss these options with mother, but she somehow never got around to reading the brochures and wasn't receptive to my suggestions of which facilities seemed most likely to be comfortable for her. Finally, I acted on what I had perhaps known all along—she didn't want to live with strangers. My partner and I talked, and decided to invite mother to join us in our home. We did, and she accepted immediately with no guise of hesitation and no restatement of her long-standing proclamation that she wouldn't live in her children's homes or interfere in their lives.

Age, experience, and my increasing research on caring, however, made me less naive than I had been when I took care of my father. I had learned that I needed to respect and care for myself as much as for others, and I resolved to give mother what I knew she would progressively need without endangering my own emotional and physical health. By this time I realized that anything short of devoting myself totally to her needs would necessarily make me uncomfortable, given how I had been socialized, so I prepared myself to endure the discomfort inherent in respecting both her needs and my own.

I need not have worried, however, for mother also had learned from our experiences caring for my father. She respected my limits, my needs, and my priorities in work and marriage. Then, too, I think her own life, which was centered on caring for all of us, made her powerfully aware of the costs of caregiving, costs she did not want to impose on my partner and me. The all-too-short fourteen-month period she lived with us before dying was one of the most transforming times of my life and, I think, of hers. Together we found ways to craft a relationship that preserved the integrity of both of us and enriched our lifelong connection.

What transpired during that time and what I continue to learn from it have profoundly changed my understanding of myself, of human relationships, and of what my work is about. I learned how to stretch for another without harming myself. I learned that responding to another's needs needn't mean forgetting my own. I learned to share another's pain without being paralyzed by it. And I learned how to ask for support from friends and family for my own pain in watching my mother die. I also had the rare opportunity to witness a kind of courage, strength, and grace that I've not seen before or since as mother bore her ever-increasing disabilities and limitations with extraordinary acceptance and sweetness. And I discovered I could count on others, particularly my partner, sister, and brother-in-law, to take care of me when I needed help. They were there for me again and again, and their support and comfort taught me additional lessons about how very important caring is. I learned, in short, that it is possible to care for others without abandoning one's self, and that caregivers, too, need to be cared for.

In addition to these personal discoveries, the experience of caring for mother accentuated larger issues about the places of care and women in our culture. One event that occurred about midway through mother's time with us recalled the conversation with my father that autumn day some years back. If what he said then had not been sufficiently clear, this second incident hammered home to me how widely endorsed is the expectation that women, not men, should make caring for others a priority in their lives.

I had arrived a few minutes early for a committee meeting on my campus. As we waited for others to arrive, three male professors and I engaged in small talk. I mentioned that I would have to leave before the committee meeting was over in order to care for mother whose regular aide was ill. Immediately they supported me with comments such as "I know it really matters to her that she's living with you"; "You're right to make time for her now while you still can"; and "Taking care of your mother is certainly more important than this meeting." I appreciated their understanding, at least until the conversation evolved further.

One of my colleagues volunteered that he had faced this issue when his mother could no longer live alone. He explained that he could not take care of her in his home and still be active professionally, so he had placed her in a nursing home. Again, there was a chorus of support for his choice: "You have to live your own life, hard as that can be"; "Well, she surely understood that as busy as you are with your work you couldn't be expected

to take on that responsibility"; and "It's true, you can't do everything; you had to put your work first."

At first I was nearly blinded by the glaring contrast between
my colleagues' assumption that I should care for my mother but
my male colleague couldn't be expected to do the same for his.
As I unfolded this brief conversation, I discovered multiple layers
of meaning. Both my male colleague and I were given certain
allowances and deprived of others—but what each of us had
was what the other lost, and what each of us lacked, the other
possessed. I was denied the right to put my work first and still
be a "good woman," and I was also given the freedom to make
caring for mother a priority. He was deprived of the right to
care for his mother and still be a "good man," and he was given
the freedom to make his work a priority. Had he made the
choice that I had, he would have been judged differently—as
unprofessional, which is to say, unmanly. Had I made the choice
he did, I would have been judged as uncaring, which is to say,
unwomanly. Both of us were the prisoners and the beneficiaries
of social expectations of women and men. Reflecting on what
that experience reveals about women, care, and culture led me
to examine these issues more fully, and that is what this book
offers.

The difference between the two times I was heavily involved
in caring for another is, in part, a difference between uninformed
and informed caring. It is also a difference between caring as
an ethical value that necessarily includes the self and caring as
a way of being for others. It is, third, a difference between caring
only for another particular person and caring about the status
of care in our culture. Finally, it is a difference between caring
because society defines it as my role as a woman and caring
in ways that challenge the very definitions that this society has
constructed for care.

It is differences such as these I hope this book helps to illuminate for others. Naturally my personal experiences found their
way into this project, as this introduction is designed to acknowledge. Yet, I think they have not led me to lapse into either a
highly subjective narrative or a sentimentalized conception of
caring.

My interest is not only—not even primarily—understanding

the issues surrounding caring for my father and mother or other relatively privileged individuals. Rather, I want to address the much larger matter of caring within our culture. What becomes of another woman who is also sixty-eight and terminally ill, but who, unlike my mother, has no relatives to care for her and no resources to pay for institutional residence? Is her only option a homeless shelter, or a curbstone if she lives in one of the many communities that have made no provisions for their homeless citizens? What becomes of the infant whose single mother works to support her, but can neither be home with her baby nor afford good day care? What becomes of the parent who requests a leave of absence from his job so he can spend a final year with his leukemia-stricken five-year-old daughter, but whose employer tells him he will be dismissed if he does so? Do we simply consign these people to the scrap heap of humanity? Do we define them as "inevitable casualties" of poverty or "shirkers who are trying to get out of work and don't deserve consideration"?

In posing these questions I point to an important theme of this book: we do, in fact, *define* what is. The poor woman and the infant are neither intrinsically worthy nor worthless, deserving of attention or disdain, inevitable or avoidable. They are what we define them as being just as caring is what we define it as being: we may designate care as something everyone deserves or as one more privilege available only to those who have status and resources in our society. Cases such as these three easily escape our notice if we limit our concerns to only those needing care within the circumference of our own personal lives. Yet to over- look human needs outside of that narrow domain is to negate the imperative that we understand caring as a cultural issue.

We must move beyond viewing caring as a strictly personal activity between individuals. Pulitzer Prize winning columnist Ellen Goodman recently observed that Americans applaud those who "pull themselves up by their own bootstraps" with only the help of family and close friends, yet many of us feel contemptu- ous of those whose success is facilitated by government assistance. Writing in 1991, Goodman asked, "What of others who may have found less help at home and need more from the govern- ment? Why is one sort of help right and the other wrong?" (13- A). Another way to ask this question is this: Why do we define legitimate care as strictly and exclusively the purview of private, personal relationships? Why is it not a concern of the whole culture? The short answer is that it isn't, because we have not defined it as a social issue. How we regard and respond to the terminally ill elderly woman, the single mother, the father wanting to be with his dying daughter depend upon how we conceive caring and its importance. In a very real sense, to paraphrase what the Queen told Alice, these people are what we say they are—nothing more and nothing less.

The central question that I raise in *Who Cares?* is, as the title suggests, who cares for others? I want to explore how discursive practices we engage in construct our views of what caring is, who cares, and what value it has. This book is an inquiry into one particular moment in our cultural attitudes toward women and caring. It is also *a* study, one of many; it is not *the* study. To attempt to resolve in a single book questions about the ways in which women and caring are and have been defined would be politically naive and intellectually foolish.

Clearly this is a very broad issue, one that has political, social, pragmatic, and philosophical aspects. Within this context I position my specific concern as discursive practices that structure culture and, thus, individuals' attitudes toward caring and women. I look to discourse not only for an explanation of how we have thus far constituted our beliefs and activities regarding caring but also for what it can suggest to us about ways we might reinvent the very social order in which we participate. I will argue that just as our individual and collective discourse has constructed the equation between women and caring so it is the primary agency through which we can redefine caring and women.

In 1982, when I first became involved significantly in caring for my father, I read a book that greatly influenced my work and my private life: Carol Gilligan's *In a Different Voice: Psychological Theory and Women's Development*. This book is an extended discourse that argues a particular view of the relationship between women and caring. Since Gilligan's effort to define women and caring is primary in my own analysis, I should introduce her work here. Gilligan argued that women's lives and senses of identities, more than those of men, are centered on relationships and on responding to others in caring ways. Although her research was limited to a very small and unrepresentative sample of women, Gilligan theorized that the "moral voice" of women

is that of caring and that women's identities are formed and
sustained in and through relationships with others.

Initially impressed by her work and others' extensions of it, I
began discussing Gilligan's ideas in my classes. I first thought,
as Gilligan did, that in praising women's tendencies to care for
others she affirmed a particular strength generally more characteristic of women than of men. I also thought that she gave
credibility to caring as a moral principle sorely undervalued in
contemporary American life.

My experiences in teaching, however, were soon to persuade
me of a quite different, potentially regressive interpretation of
Gilligan's ideas. As I taught her views about care, I saw my women
students embracing Gilligan's description of woman's role as
caregiver and finding in it legitimation of their devotion to others,
even when that entailed severe sacrifices in personal health, opportunities, and identities. The men in my classes responded in
a different, yet quite consistent way. As one young man said,
"I'm really glad women do all of that stuff, because I wouldn't
be very good at it. Besides, it would take time away from the
real priorities in my life." Another student, an older man, commented, "I don't know what I'd do if my wife didn't keep up
with the kids and take care of them or didn't remember my
family's birthdates and anniversaries—probably the family would
just fall apart. I really count on her to keep all of that off of me
so I can do my work." It's significant that the second comment
was from a man whose wife was employed full time in her own
demanding career.

In these comments and many others like them what I heard
was not new, but old; it was all too familiar. Women are expected
to care for others—to do the caring, in fact, for the whole society.
Gilligan, I realized, was a distinctly conservative voice, one that
accepts the given organization of Western culture and the sex
roles inherent in that. Her work clearly affirms the importance
of caring, yet it just as clearly reinforces caring's traditional association with women. Her ideas, as my students and a number of
critics pointed out, buttress age-old stereotypes of both sexes.
Women are defined as nurturers, the people who provide comfort, compassion, and care. Men, meanwhile, go about doing the
"important stuff."

The men in my classes saw Gilligan's arguments as justifying their lack of involvement in others' lives and lack of responsibility for caring for others, while the women saw her ideas as legitimizing their continued focus on others, often at the cost of their own interests. Clearly, this result was not what I had intended; I also think Gilligan did not anticipate her work would be used to support conclusions that reinforce limiting sex roles, separating women from autonomous pursuits and men from relationships with others.

I then began a more intensive study of Gilligan's work to better understand what she wrote and why it could lead to interpretations that restrict the development and experience of both women and men. As I reread her work, along with increasing criticism of it, I realized that her account of care is incomplete in important respects. What seems missing in her work is an understanding of the ways in which care has been historically situated. Because caring has traditionally been performed by women, there has arisen a tacit equation between womanliness and providing care.

It is this deeply entrenched cultural assumption that women do and should demonstrate care in order to be feminine or womanly that renders the injunction to care potentially paralyzing for women, one that threatens their selfhood. Because Gilligan's account isolates caring from the historical contexts from which its meaning has been constructed, her advocacy of women's caring emerges as both naive and potentially regressive for women.

While Gilligan acknowledges that caring for others is not a priority in our society and that women's involvement in caring puts them at risk, she dismisses these issues as "society's problem." She proceeds to argue that women should affirm and cultivate their tendencies to care for others based on the intrinsic merit of caring. Yet, to ask women to continue to be the caregivers in a culture that devalues both caring and those who engage in it is to invite them to participate in their own subordination.

What Gilligan does not do is situate care within the culture and, relatedly, focus on structural changes that have potential to alter the social meaning of care in ways that make it something both men and women may engage in without excessive losses in autonomy and status. Gilligan, then, reflects and contributes to a particular discursive tradition, one which hearkens back at least to classical Greece: life is divided into public and private spheres, men and women are placed respectively within them, and differential values are assigned to each, the public being the more important in the life of a culture.

In this book, I continue the work that Gilligan launched by offering a fuller account of caring as it has been historically situated and defined. This entails, on one hand, locating caring for others within the particular historical, cultural, social, economic, and personal contexts in which it has occurred and through which its meaning has been constructed, and, on the other hand, focusing on symbolic and structural forces that sustain meanings which marginalize caring in Western society. I argue that it is possible to redefine what caring means in ways that free it from its historical placement and make it both safe and rewarding for all of us—women and men alike—to care for others without some of the exorbitant costs it has historically exacted from women. I regard this as one of the most universal and important urgencies facing us as individuals and as a nation.

Seven chapters and a short conclusion comprise this book. In chapter 2, I establish the rationale for my inquiry by examining the crisis of care facing contemporary Western culture. I then introduce the framework for my inquiry by discussing the central ideas of caring and women and the ways in which both and the relationship between them have been discursively constituted.

In chapter 3, I further explore the relationship that has been culturally constructed between women and caring and how it often poses excessive costs for women who care for others.

I offer in chapter 4 a sustained analysis of one key text, Gilligan's *In a Different Voice*, in the current debate about women and caring. Here I try to reveal both how her text works persuasively and why it is a flawed or incomplete understanding of caring in Western culture.

In chapter 5, I pursue a fuller account of caring by examining the kinds of explanations offered for the tendency to care for others. This analysis reveals that caring is a highly complex set of attitudes and activities that arise out of diverse motives and historical circumstances and are then represented in discursive practices that maintain associations among women, caring, subordination, and the private sphere.

The idea of discourse as a primary means of creating social

organization is discussed in chapter 6 and, with that, the values, institutions, and practices that comprise social life.

Finally, in chapter 7, I consider the future of caring in the United States by pointing to some of the structural changes required if caring is to be redefined in ways that are life affirming for the culture and those who choose to care for others. What I call for is nothing short of a transformation in certain values; I believe anything less will be insufficient for us if we are to build a future of quality for ourselves as individuals and a society.

The closing chapter weaves together themes developed in previous chapters to underline connections between cultural structures and practices and the work of providing care.

We urgently need to revise long-standing but outmoded views of caring as a strictly private matter and of women as the ones who should care for others. I hope *Who Cares?* is persuasive in its effort to demonstrate that these views and the social organization that grows out of them are no longer workable. The social model that defined caring as a responsibility of individuals and families that was perhaps workable, albeit inequitable, in the 1950s, doesn't fit the 1990s, and it is entirely off the mark for what will face us as we move into the next century. This obsolete model is inadequate to provide human, humane responses to the rapidly accelerating number of people who need care.

I also hope this book will increase awareness of structural obstacles and symbolic practices that currently hinder our abilities to provide reasonable care for others without suffering unreasonable losses ourselves.

The average American woman will spend seventeen years raising children and eighteen years helping aged parents.
　　　　　　　　　　　　　　—Melinda Beck et al., *Newsweek*

How we live our lives as conscious thinking subjects, and how we give meaning to the material social conditions under which we live and which structure our everyday lives, depends on the range and social power of existing discourses, our access to them, and the political strength of the interests they represent.
　　—C. Weedon, *Feminist Practice and Poststructuralist Theory*

CHAPTER 2
Who Cares in Contemporary Western Culture?

Who Cares? is about caring, women, and the discourse that comprises contemporary American culture. These concerns are closely connected, and it is their interrelationship that I seek to explore in this book. Caring, an activity consistently graced with more lip service than actual respect, has become at once a more urgent and more controversial issue in our social contract. It has become more pressing because our needs for caregivers are growing rapidly; it has become more controversial and difficult to address because many who traditionally have engaged in both normal and extraordinary caring for others are beginning to challenge the expectation that they will or should be more responsible for providing care than other members of the culture. Specifically, women, who historically have been the primary caregivers in the United States, no longer uncritically and uniformly accept that responsibility. Within the lives that many contemporary women lead there is not adequate time and energy to be the sole providers of good care for family and friends.

Discourse comprises the principal means whereby we as individuals and a culture define values, roles, activities, goals, and status, to name but a few of the phenomena whose meaning arises out of communication carried on throughout a society. Among the phenomena named and defined by cultural discourse are women and the importance of caring for others. As Weedon (1987) reminds us, "Language is the place where actual and possible forms of social and political consequences are defined and contested. Yet, it is also the place where our sense of ourselves, our subjectivity, is constructed" (21). It is through language that we construct meanings for caring, women, men, and public and private concerns, and it is in and through communication that we sustain or alter the meanings into which we have entered. Thus, to study ourselves and the practices of our culture we must look closely at our language.

In this chapter I introduce each of these key terms and begin to trace their interrelationships in order to provide a preview of the book as a whole, which attempts to inquire into the personal, political, and social implications of caring in American culture as revealed in and constructed by discursive practices in our culture.

In this book I blend reflections on personal experiences with reports from others who have been involved in giving care and who have studied and thought seriously about the place of care in our society. My inquiry is an effort to answer the question, who cares? I want to know why some people—more often women—care for others, how they come to have that inclination and the skills required to act upon it, and what caring for others does to and for caretakers. Simultaneously and inevitably I am inquiring into how our culture defines caring for others and women's roles in that activity and whether this understanding is enhancing for individuals and the social order or whether it can be re-formed to meet more adequately the growing needs for care in contemporary America.

A First Look at Caring and Women in the United States

Interest in caring or caregiving is not new. It is basic to any form of civilized life. All societies define what kinds and levels of care are to be expected and then devise systems for ensuring such care is provided. Typically, cultures designate particular members or groups as caregivers and then specify the status that role will have in the culture. Socializing new members into a culture is largely a process of convincing them to accept socially constructed definitions and roles as "natural" and "right" descriptions of the way things are. As with other cultural phenomena, this has been the case with caring (Janeway, 1971; Miller, 1986).

What is new are questions about how our culture defines who is to care and, equally important, the values our culture attaches to caregiving activities and the people who are implicitly or explicitly charged to engage in them. In recent years, particularly the last decade, questions about caregiving—and more specifically women's prominent role in caregiving—have resulted in considerable debate in and beyond academe (Berg, 1986; Brody, 1985; Faludi, 1991; Friedan, 1981; Okin, 1989; Stoller, 1983; Tavris, 1992).

From this discourse two extreme positions have emerged. One viewpoint, often assumed by politically liberal individuals as well as both socialist and capitalist feminists, argues that women have been assigned virtually exclusive responsibility for taking care of others. It is also claimed by those holding this position that caregiving is not highly valued by the society as a whole, that is, it is not accorded substantial status or prestige and is not adorned with symbols that reflect valuation, specifically salary and prestige. Thus, goes the argument, women continuing to be the primary caregivers in contemporary Western society serves to perpetuate their already subordinate place within a hegemonic social order that requires but does not value or reward caregiving (Blum, Homiak, Housman, & Scheman, 1976; Hare-Mustin & Marecek, 1990; Kerber, 1986).

To remain in a role that is broadly devalued erodes self-esteem. "If society stamps you as a second-class citizen, how can you trust or value yourself highly?" asks Janeway (1971, 111). And if women don't value themselves because they understand what they're expected to do isn't valued by the culture, then it is difficult to build the kind of strength and sense of one's own entitlements required to challenge either how the culture defines care or its designation of certain people as caregivers. This analysis can and often does lead to the conclusion that women should not continue to assume primary responsibility for caring for others.

A second position, often assumed by revalorizing feminists as well as politically and socially traditional individuals, holds that caregiving is an essential and sacred activity for which women are particularly well suited and at which they are particularly skilled. This argument entails a view of women as having a kind of essential goodness, purity, compassion, empathy, and/or other qualities that set them apart from men and suit them naturally to attending to others (Dupré, 1990). This latter position has been reinvigorated by much work in the past decade, including a particularly influential book that appeared in 1982. In this publication, Carol Gilligan identified caring as a moral concern that has been suppressed in Western culture and is particularly heard in the voices of women. According to Gilligan, our culture values fairness over caring and equates the former with moral maturity. Perhaps more than any other modern writer had done, Gilligan championed women's tendencies to care, referring to this as "woman's place in man's life cycle" (17). She urged women to continue caring, secure in the knowledge that it is a worthy activity, regardless of whether the surrounding culture recognizes and rewards it as such.

Within this tradition Nel Noddings has emerged as a major supporter of the position Gilligan advanced. Noddings (1990) argues that "the construction of ethics from the standpoint of women is an important enterprise that may contribute significantly to both ethical thinking and general human welfare" (161). Like Gilligan, Noddings dismisses cultural devaluations of caring as uninformed and advocates caring as intrinsically worthy: "The one caring, then, is unquestionably awarded . . . 'moral worth,' for by definition . . . [this person] is capable of the most significant form of human response—caring" (173). Thus, Noddings, Gilligan, and others who align themselves with this second position suggest that caring for others is something women have always done and should continue doing. Caring, they maintain, should be a source of pleasure and satisfaction despite the lack of regard bestowed on it by the surrounding culture.

As I indicated earlier, these are only two positions, albeit two particularly visible ones, in a topic of growing interest. Clearly much territory lies between the extremes of these stances, so it's hardly surprising that other perspectives are being articulated and incorporated into the ongoing cultural conversation about caring. Dealing with the question of who cares has become increasingly salient as those who need care increase and those willing to provide it do not. It has also become exceedingly complex since asking who cares involves questioning deeply entrenched assumptions about ourselves as individuals and our priorities as a society.

It is between these extreme positions that perhaps the majority of Americans find themselves, be they homemakers, brick masons, attorneys, teachers, mine workers, or doctors. Most people recognize the need for caregiving in contexts ranging from child-rearing to institutional life to caring for elderly, often ill, individuals. Most Americans realize care should be, must be, available if children are to grow up healthy and productive, if the mentally and/or physically ill are to have any chance to recover, and if our elderly are to be given dignity and comfort in the final stages of their lives. We want care to be provided for them and—in time—for ourselves.

Yet, difficult and persistent questions follow from that general consensus. Who is to bestow the care most of us agree is needed? How are we as a culture to define the worth of caring for others? Whom do we expect to provide patience, support, kindness, comfort, understanding, and acceptance of physical and/or mental problems? Whom do we ask to take responsibility for caring for others? Whose time do we take for these vital activities? How do we regard and reward those involved in caring for others? How do we justify assumptions that it is acceptable or right to expect only certain people or classes of people to arrange their lives in order to care for others?

The answer that has worked historically in the United States has become problematical in recent times. Traditionally, it was the role of the family, and particularly of women within it, to care for others. Families took care of their children when young, their elderly when old, and their sick and disabled when necessary; within families, the primary hands-on tasks of caregiving traditionally fell to women. Men, so the old adage goes, were the head of families and women the heart.[1]

Yet, many Western women no longer accept the traditional expectation that caring for others should be their primary responsibility or life focus. Today, 67 percent of women with children under three years of age work outside of their homes. In addition to single mothers who obviously need to earn incomes, there are many married women who work outside of their homes either as an individual preference or because two salaries are needed to maintain an acceptable standard of living. Who cares for the children of this 67 percent of mothers? Certainly not the government: of all of the developed countries in the world, America provides the least support for child care and child rearing (Hewlett, 1986, 1991).

The report of the National Commission on Children, issued in June of 1991, persuasively documents the jeopardy faced by America's children, because they are not receiving sufficient care in their homes, schools, communities, and nation. We wince in reading the conclusions of this blue-ribbon panel, but what can we do? Who is to provide the care these children so desperately need if they are to develop strong minds, hearts, and spirits?

So far the de facto answer has been that women still do the great majority of caring for children and elderly parents or in-laws, and many of them do this in addition to working, usually full time, outside of the home. *American Demographics* reported in 1988 that men in two-worker families had finally assumed substantial responsibility for taking care of children and the home; that responsibility, however, amounted to ten hours for the woman's twenty—half as much. Hochschild's (1989) study of two-worker families found that only twenty percent of husbands in two-worker families shared childrearing and homemaking tasks equally with their wives. Regardless of the level and responsibilities of their jobs outside the home, women are still overwhelmingly more likely than men to take time off from work to care for a sick child (Okin, 1989) or elderly relative (Beck et al., 1990; Halpern, 1987; Sommers & Shields, 1987).

In her analysis of women's roles Janeway (1971) concludes that "mothering is the area where questioning of woman's role has made least impact" (149). Whatever questions have been raised about fairness have "not led to a change in the fundamental social fact that women bring up children. . . . So it has been, and so it is" (149). Janeway is quite correct on two counts: first, she correctly notes that women still assume the overwhelming responsibility of caring for children, and, second, she calls attention to recognizing this arrangement is a "social fact," not an absolute "truth" dictated by biology or other unchangeable factors. The cultural mythology still holds that mothers, more than fathers, should be responsible for their children. Unlike father-hood, motherhood is normatively defined in large part by con-crete, constant activities of caring.

"Women are told that a great deal has changed," writes Barbara Berg (1986) in the opening paragraph of her book, "but upon closer look, the scope of the change is not what it seems" (17). Meanwhile, *Newsweek* (Beck et al., 1990) reports that "while women have become a major force in the American workplace, their roles as caregivers remain entrenched in the expectations of society and individual families" (47). Psychology professor James Halpern (1987) concurs, noting that women are the ones who do the vast majority of childcare—and care in general—for the whole society. The traditional pattern and sex roles, in short, are still in place, but they are getting ragged at the edges.

This pattern is neither healthy for nor acceptable to many women today. Hochschild (1989) reports that resentment and deep fatigue are major costs of women's extra caregiving respon-sibilities, costs which jeopardize marital harmony and women's psychological and physical well being. Caring for children and the home, then, is a major point of tension in contemporary relationships in our country. This tension, growing in correspon-dence with the number of women who work and have children, is one of the forces pushing the issue of who cares to the forefront of the American agenda.

And what of the elderly? Who is to care for them? This question takes on new urgency now that medical technology has so radi-cally extended the human life span. At the turn of the century the average life span was a mere 47 years. Today the average American woman can expect to live 78.5 years, and the average American man can expect to live 71.8 years—slightly less for African Americans, slightly more for Caucasians. At the 1992 annual conference of the American Association for the Advance-ment of Science, it was reported that by 2050 there will be more than twice as many Americans over 65 as there are today—a rise of 42 million—and over 15 million will live beyond age 85. These elderly people will not be able to take care of all of their own practical and/or medical needs. They will require help.

Should they be put in institutions, as nearly 2 million older adults are today? Or should they join the families of their adult children, who are often in the midst of raising their own children? Aging parents' needs often come at a time when their children have the greatest responsibility for their own children or just when the children's children have left home and the parents are looking forward to their first years of being able to focus primarily on their individual and couple lives. Dubbed the "sandwich generation" by *Newsweek* (Beck et al., 1990) in a recent cover story, many middle-aged people today find themselves caught between caring for their young and their elderly family members. Jesse Benjamin of the Bureau of Labor Statistics calls it the "double whammy," caught between childcare and eldercare (Beck et al., 1990, 47). Must we be caught in an intergenerational war in which we're forced to choose between caring for our young and our old or trying to do both at whatever personal costs? Is this really the best answer that we as a society can generate?

When we examine who cares for the elderly, we find that, once again, it is the women in families who do the direct caregiving: the wives, daughters, daughters-in-law, sisters, and aunts. *Newsweek* (Beck et al., 1990) reports that "three-fourths of those caring for the elderly are women, as it has always been" (45). Since nearly half of these women have full-time jobs outside of their homes, caring for elderly relatives is usually an added responsibility (Halpern, 1987; Stoller, 1983). Many women shop, cook, and clean for their parents before and after work, use their lunch hours to run their parents' errands, and give up weekends with their husbands and children to be with parents. Some find they cannot "do it all," and they quit their jobs or work only part-time to free time and energy to take care of parents (Beck et al., 1990; Berg, 1986; Halpern, 1987; Stoller, 1983). In other cases— some seventy thousand—the elderly are abandoned by their families (Goodman, 1992).

Just a few years ago Sommers and Shields (1987) reported that 80 to 90 percent of elderly Americans were not living in nursing homes and depended on family members to care for them. Their study of older Americans revealed that almost always it is female members of the family who provide care. Even when a male is more closely related and/or more geographically near, it tends to be some woman in a family that assumes the responsibility of caring while others seldom even question the assumption

that she will and should. Again, the responsibility of caring for
others falls to women; again, women accept it. Research by Aronson (1992), Berg (1986), and Halpern (1987) shows that both
women and men feel caring for others is more "the woman's
job," while *Newsweek* (Beck et al., 1990) reports that "many husbands are unable—or unwilling—to confront the emotional demands of elder care, even when the aged parents are their own"
(47).

Clearly, the association between women and caring is neither
absolute nor complete. There are women who do not seem particularly oriented toward caring for others, so we cannot say that
all women are involved in giving care. Likewise, there are many
men who do give care and who derive great satisfaction from
their ability to nurture and comfort others. These qualifications
are necessary in discussing the relationship between women and
care. Nonetheless, it is indisputable that in Western culture dramatically more women than men devote substantial portions of
their lives to caring for others. Because this is and has always
been true, it becomes important to ask why women as a group
are the primary caregivers of society and why men as a group
have been excluded and excused from the responsibilities and
the growth inherent in caring for others.

While women still provide the majority of care for children,
elderly family members, and people in general, they no longer
do so without comment or question. A number of critical voices
have called attention to the inequity of women who are expected
to work a "second shift" (Hochschild, 1989): one shift at work
outside of the home and a second one in the home. Why is it,
ask critics like Hochschild, Sommers and Shield (1987), and Okin
(1989), in a time where women generally have substantial work
responsibilities outside of the home that society still expects
women (and women expect themselves) to do the great majority
of caring for others? And why, whether done by a family member
or a paid worker, is caregiving not highly regarded, recognized,
or rewarded in our society? Why are the "caring professions"
notorious for having among the lowest salaries in our country?

These questions are difficult ones for all of us. Often they are
especially difficult for women to pose, since to ask them is to
suggest they themselves don't value giving care or even don't
value others who need care. "It's hard for women to strike against

the double day," Snitow (1990) recently pointed out. "It may feel too much like striking against our own children" (84). It may seem selfish to a woman to ask whether taking care of a child or an ailing parent or in-law should require so much of *her* time. Drawing on years of experience counseling women, Miller (1986) observes, "Women constantly confront themselves with questions about giving. Am I giving enough? Can I give enough? Why don't I give enough? They frequently have deep fears about what this must mean about them. They are upset if they feel they are not givers" (50). The firmly ensconced cultural view of women as givers creates an injunction that women *must be* givers to be good women. This can lead, as Miller observes, to women's feeling guilty if they don't give freely and fully of themselves to anyone who needs help.

Miller also reports that "outside of the clinical setting, most women do not even dare to suggest openly such a possibility" that they might not care for others (50). Most women realize how deeply settled is the cultural expectation that women will give and how closely fulfilling that expectation is linked to evaluations of their worth as women. If a woman voices reservations about whether she should be expected to take care of others, she is likely to get responses, implicit or explicit, that reveal disapproval, perhaps condemnation, of her selfishness—a cardinal sin given prevailing images of women. If others do not give such responses (or are not invited to as when a woman doesn't ask the question), then women may well criticize themselves for their feelings. Like other members of the culture, they have internalized the belief that women should be compassionate and caring: they find themselves caught in what Sommers and Shields (1987) call the "compassion trap" in which women feel they must be compassionate, caring, tender and must be so without complaint or even inner resentment. Not to be so is not to be a woman—this remains largely true in our country even in the 1990s.

Even when others' demands become excessive and interfere seriously with women's personal and professional lives and often their health, Miller (1986) observes that "they cannot even allow themselves to admit that they resent these excess pressures. . . . Consequently, they cannot let themselves openly call a halt to the demands or even take small steps to limit them" (51). Rowbotham

(1973) points out that women's socialization highlights self-denial as the ideal of womanhood, which leads to the paradox that many women can only affirm themselves by denying themselves! To put their needs and goals ahead of or even equal to those of others would be to run afoul of the cultural definition of what women are and should be.

Yet, the difficult question of who cares is not a "woman's issue." Clearly the need for care affects all of us. Further, all of us participate in defining what care is, how much is to be provided, and who is to give it. Although caring historically has been expected of and performed by women more than men, this is not a necessary and certainly not an immutable association. Dealing with the question of who cares, then, is the business of all who comprise our culture and participate in establishing and sustaining its meanings.

Our efforts to wrestle with this problem frequently land us in our own contradictions. On the one hand, most people do not openly disparage giving care. In fact, most people, when asked, claim they think caring for others is part of what it means to have a humane society. On the other hand, most people don't want to have to be the ones to give care; often they refuse to support funding required to provide care as evident in opposition to taxes that would improve schools, clinics, day care, social services, and the variety of other institutionalized ways of assisting those in need.

The reluctance to give care and the substantial lack of support for programs that might provide a degree of help to those in need reveal the widely shared understanding that giving care is not valued by the existing social order and, thus, those who do it are not valued. In the summer of 1991, to take just one particular demonstration of how cultural values are expressed, our government trimmed defense spending only minimally while eviscerating funding for a number of educational and social programs. Some states had to reduce or entirely eliminate even the most basic support for indigent elderly and homeless citizens, but money for new military weapons was preserved.

Reflecting on these budget decisions, child development expert Mary Wright Edleman (1991) perceptively asks, "If political leaders don't blink about bailing out savings-and-loan institutions to the tune of at least $160 billion, or spending $1 billion a day on the Persian Gulf War, why should we blink about insisting that they bail children and families out of poverty at a cost of $20 billion annually?" (76). Budget appropriations offer but one example of what our culture does and does not value and how it communicates that valuation through concrete actions and policies.

As a society, then, we find ourselves in the most uncomfortable dilemma of desiring, even requiring something we are not willing to recognize as valuable and to reward accordingly. Specifically, we do not demonstrate that care is valued through substantial funding, material rewards, and symbolic status, the primary means of declaring worth in capitalistic culture.

Neither do we provide the kinds of even minimal support that would make it easier for people to care for others. Business and industry have done nothing systematic to accommodate the needs of working parents (Hewlett, 1986, 1991). To date, only 3 percent of companies in the United States offer any kind of assistance to employees caring for elderly relatives (Beck et al., 1990, 46); there are no tax reductions or subsidies for elderly care (Silverstone & Hyman, 1989). Indeed, as Halpern (1987) sardonically observes, "Although children in our society honor their parents, it sometimes seems that government does not" (248).

To argue against caregiving—or even to argue that this should not be so consistently and virtually the exclusive province of women—can seem hard-hearted and distinctly unfeminine. Yet, within the existing cultural system of values, to agree that caring is important and women should continue to engage in it may cement the very kinds of impediments that have historically deprived women of the personal and professional freedom required to participate equally in individual, civic, and professional pursuits (Faludi, 1991; Kerber, 1986; Okin, 1989). Equally important but far less recognized is the fact that to continue to assign caring to women excludes men from important avenues of personal development (Halpern, 1987; Miller, 1986).

Ironically, the very gains of the second wave of feminism have contributed to the increased need for care and the simultaneous decreased willingness of women to provide it. This does not suggest that women or the women's movement are somehow to blame for accelerating problems in providing supervision, assistance, and companionship to children and elderly people.

Rather, the progress that has been made reconfigures the culture and, with it, the kinds of needs that emerge and assumptions about how those are to be met. This is precisely the point of Friedan's (1981) book, *The Second Stage*, in which she argues, "There is no going back. The women's movement was necessary. But the liberation that began with the women's movement isn't finished. The equality we fought for isn't livable, isn't workable, isn't comfortable" (40).

As women have won access to equal education, minimum protection against discrimination in the workplace, and greater economic and social freedom, they have realized the benefits of status and material rewards that come with those opportunities. They have found a new truth in those proclaimed in the Declaration of Sentiments delivered at the Seneca Falls Convention in 1848: "We hold these truths to be self-evident: that all men and women are created equal; that they are endowed by their Creator with certain inalienable rights; that among these are life, liberty and the pursuit of happiness; that to secure these rights governments are instituted, deriving their just powers from the consent of the governed" (Stanton, Anthony, & Gage, 1881–1886, 1:70).

The early suffragists asked for no more or less than men enjoyed as rights and opportunities. It took nearly a century, however, before any of the real freedoms and rights Stanton and her colleagues envisioned were to be enjoyed by substantial numbers of women. During the past couple of decades many women have pursued educational and work activities, and often they have discovered that worklife can be rewarding, that being admired and respected for what our society defines as "productive labor" is gratifying, that individual challenges and pursuits can be enlarging and exciting, and that one's own salary offers an unparalleled degree of not just economic security but social and personal as well. Not surprisingly, many women are reluctant to give up these hard won freedoms and return to the precarious security and low respect accorded to traditional roles for women.

Self-appointed social critics, it is true, often claim that a great many current social problems such as broken homes, latch-key children, and poor performance in schools are the result of women's having the audacity and the selfishness to abandon their roles in the home. This kind of argument folds in on itself as one realizes the vested interest of the arguer in having women stay in the home. All social arrangements serve some interest; thus, the question is always *whose* interests are served by women's primacy in the context of caregiving: men's interests? families' interests?

Blaming women also begs the larger question of how society should be constituted. If one assumes that traditional roles are "right" in some sense—whether because of divine law, commitment to tradition, or innate capabilities—then it follows that women have stepped out of place and out of line by participating in the world beyond the home. Clearly, there is considerable support for this viewpoint in contemporary America. Faludi's (1991) recent *Backlash* documents Berg's earlier report that during the last decade there has been a "re-emergence of conservative attitudes nationwide . . . [toward] reaffirming the values of individualism and of traditional family life and gender roles" (18).[2]

Yet, we cannot afford to reaffirm traditions uncritically. We cannot reasonably expect our lives in the 1990s to be guided by values and ideals of the 1950s. There are real questions to be asked about how we should constitute the social order itself so that it is workable in our era. As soon as we broach these questions, we invite reassessment of social roles as they have been defined historically and social organization as it has operated in the past. In later chapters I return to this issue to explore some alternative ways in which we might organize our culture and the roles and activities comprising it. For now, however, it's sufficient to realize that the social order and its incumbent roles are constructed and, thus, can be variously reconstructed. This leads to the question of how a culture defines itself and its members, and that inevitably leads us to discourse.

Discourse and the Construction of Culture

A culture defines its priorities, the roles of its members, and its overall organization through discourse. This is to say that it is in and through communication that we come to understand our own nature as well as what different interests, activities, and feelings mean and for whom they are "appropriate." Writing of this, Chris Weedon (1987) argues that "the nature of femininity and masculinity is one of the key sites of discursive struggle for

the individual" (98). The nature of each gender—what it means
to be a woman or man—is currently hotly contested. Again,
consider Weedon's argument that "there are currently several
conflicting accounts . . . which inform different common-sense
assumptions about women's subjectivity and social role. . . . Each
of these accounts is competing for the meaning [of "woman"]
. . . in ways which imply not only different social and political
consequences for women, but also the different forms of feminine subjectivity which are the precondition for meaningful action" (26–27). Concurring with Weedon is Broughton (1983)
who observes that "gender is fundamentally a symbolic issue . . .
interpreted anew in each generation" (641–642). What we understand "man" and "woman" to mean, then, depends closely on
how they are symbolized within our culture.

   Yet, as both Weedon and Broughton recognize, precisely because there is no monolithic, universal view of the sexes, no view
that is not historically variable, the culture's definitions of men
and women as well as our own senses of ourselves are open
to change. When such change does occur, it occurs through
discursive encounters. It is in and through our interactions with
language that we come to understand how others perceive themselves and us and that we arrive at definitions, always tentative,
of ourselves and the kinds of activities, goals, attitudes, and values
we embrace. According to Weedon, it is in "discourses in circula-
tion at any particular moment that we are offered subject positions which assume what it is to be a woman or man and which
seek to constitute our femininity and masculinity accordingly"
(100).

   Weedon and others who focus on the relationship between
discursive practices and cultural beliefs offer an especially rich
understanding of how interaction within a culture constitutes
social order. It is conversation between individuals, arguments
among policy makers, broadcasts of addresses, lectures in class-
rooms, conferences in corporate boardrooms, speeches from
public platforms and pulpits, and, importantly, written texts including letters, formal documents, magazines, and books. In fact,
Weedon points out that "literature is one specific site among
many where the ideological construction of gender takes place.
. . . Literature, like other forms of discourse, is concerned to

construct apparently 'natural' ways of being a woman or man" (167).

Following Weedon's lead, I look to discourse as one site where we may identify and evaluate competing constructions of both women and the relationship between women and caring. I will focus intensively on one particular discourse and the responses it has occasioned from a variety of people. Carol Gilligan's book, *In A Different Voice: Psychological Theory and Women's Development*, published in 1982, is a particularly appropriate work to study since it has had inordinate impact on both academic and popular thought and, particularly, on views of women and their association with caring. It is also appropriate because it represents many of the issues and arguments comprising general controversy about caring and gender roles. From the start, Gilligan's book generated controversy; thus, it and responses to it comprise a valuable focus for examining how discursive practices craft and argue about images of women and their roles in caring for others.

Unfortunately, discourse about these issues has not been consistently informed nor has it invariably increased understanding of various concerns, positions, and options. In some cases, voices have been strident, accusatory, and dogmatic; too often advocates of a position have not considered alternative stances as an opportunity to reflect and, perhaps, to modify their own views; too frequently discourse has been punctuated by caricatures. Acrimony has sometimes displaced thoughtful deliberation; protecting one's own position has overshadowed attempts to understand other perspectives within the debate.

I enter this dialogue as a critic with my own particular, provisional position in order to study how various discourses work and for what they argue. My goal is neither to adopt the divisive tone of much contemporary discourse about caregiving in America nor to "prove" the rightness or wrongness of particular claims about women's role in the process of caring for others. Instead, I hope to enlarge understanding of the grounds of the debate, the issues that are at stake, and the ramifications of various answers to the pivotal question: who cares? Toward this end, I examine caregiving as both a concrete activity and a socially constructed practice, and I reflect on the consequences of each of these.

Realizing that care, like any human activity, is constructed through the discourses of a culture directs our attention to cultural sites within which limiting conceptions of care can be challenged and changed. By identifying locations where views of caring and women may be redefined, and by assuming a voice in those places, we advance simultaneously the possibilities that we can ameliorate many of the exorbitant personal costs to individuals who do provide care, involve a greater diversity of people in the activities of caring, and create a more humane and life affirming culture for us all.

"She never thought of herself, always took care of others, the most selfless person I've ever known. She really was a good woman."

"She was the quiet glue that held everyone else together. She made their lives possible as only a woman can."

CHAPTER 3
Women, Caring, and the Burden of Selflessness

These comments, at my mother's funeral last year, provoked conflicting feelings in me. In one sense what these people said was absolutely right. Yet, just as strongly, it seemed wrong that these were the summaries of my mother's life. I admired and had clearly benefited from her years of selfless care, yet I also mourned her long before she died; I mourned the self she'd sacrificed to be such a "good woman."

Why was mother's identity only a footnote to her family's life? Why did these people at her funeral describe her only in terms of what she had done for others? What had happened to her in her own right? What became of the girl who was so intelligent she was pushed ahead three years in elementary school, the teenager who had the courage and strength of her convictions to convert to Catholicism over the intense objections of her very Protestant parents, the woman who got a Bachelor of Science degree in business administration at a time when few women went to college and fewer still pursued studies in business, the adventurous spirit who enlisted in the Waves during World War II, the person with enough ambition and ability to become the first woman stockbroker in North Carolina?

Where had that woman gone? How had so many of her abilities and ambitions been eclipsed by the roles of wife and mother? From infrequent stories and photographs I knew about that woman, but I could never see her in my mother. Why in our

forty-year relationship had I never known but only known of
the woman who did all of those things? Why had she abandoned
that self?

Reflecting on the comments I'd heard at mother's funeral, I
thought back on the past fourteen months when mom had lived
with my husband and me, gracing our home with her quiet,
unassuming presence. I recalled our trips to her doctor and later,
when she could no longer travel, his visits to our home. I used
to encourage her to press him to explain his advice in ordinary
language nonspecialists could understand and to initiate conversation about issues that concerned her, but she repeatedly told
me she didn't feel she could do that—she felt she had no right
to question him. How could someone who at twenty-two had
possessed the intelligence and ambition to be a naval intelligence
officer during wartime be the same person who at sixty-seven
felt she would be out of place to ask legitimate questions of her
doctor?

Again I replayed the comments I had heard. Intended as
praise of her goodness and virtue, the speakers' remarks also
revealed their assumptions of what a "good woman" is. Of course,
they weren't simply expressing their opinions as particular individuals. What they said inevitably reflected beliefs of the culture
within which these speakers were situated and from which they
drew their understandings of what things mean. The ideas these
individuals voiced reflect widely endorsed cultural beliefs about
womanhood, beliefs that are reinforced, recreated as individuals
give voice to them. In this instance, the speakers and their statements emanate from a deeply entrenched cultural conception
of women in which caring for others is equated with goodness,
in which the extreme of that—selflessness—is also the ideal of
womanhood.

The equation of womanly goodness with giving to others is long
established in Western culture. Linda Kerber (1986), a historian,
traces it all the way back to classical Greece, where men were
assumed to be more interested in and skilled at participating in
civic life and the public arena, while women were understood to
realize themselves most fully through caring for others in the
domestic realm (306). In the United States this view of women
not only held sway as the "cult of true womanhood" in the 1800s
(Kerber, 1986) but also as the dominant cultural ideal of feminin-

ity in the mid 1900s. For example, in an article in *Life* magazine in 1956, Coughlan stated, "Women have minds and should use them . . . so long as their primary interest and activity is the home" (110), a particularly ironic comment given the title of the article: "Changing Roles in Modern Marriage"! We might appropriately ask what has changed and what is modern in Coughlan's point of view. The ideal of women as selfless and dedicated to family continues to resonate in our times. In her analysis of meanings of femininity, Rosenblum (1989) finds evidence that currently powerful "normative injunctions which prescribe self-sacrifice as evidence of femininity" are present throughout Western civilization. She demonstrates their presence in contexts from "the early nineteenth century 'cult of true womanhood,'. . . to contemporary working women concerned to show that their employment benefits their family rather than themselves . . . and even to the concentration of women workers in the service sector of the labor force, femininity has both been equated with and displayed by care for others rather than self" (196). The normative injunctions Rosenblum identifies are not only in the society in general. They are also central to the more personal processes of socialization in individual families.

Describing the activities that go into mothering a daughter, a number of authors have highlighted the importance of teaching young girls to be sensitive and giving to others—to be, in short, caring. In their discussion of raising girls, Eichenbaum and Orbach (1983b), for instance, note the importance of teaching them "to provide nurturance, care and attention. . . . Firstly, mothers need to prepare their daughters to become givers. . . . Consciously and unconsciously, then, mothers encourage and reinforce a daughter's moves to be caring, to develop her emotional radar, to be responsive. Mothers tell their daughters not to be selfish, . . . to pay attention to others' needs" (47). We should also note that parents do not routinely emphasize selflessness, caring, and responsiveness in raising sons.

There is, in fact, considerable evidence to suggest that the ideal of woman as selfless, giving, nurturing, and focused on others is resurging in contemporary life. Indicative of this is the resounding response to Gilligan's work (1982), which portrayed women as guided by a desire to care for others. Her widely read and embraced book and the substantial work inspired by it have done much to revitalize the cultural assumption that caring for and giving to others should be *the* priorities in women's lives. So my mother had lived out the imperatives of womanliness as defined by Gilligan and a host of others before and since. And the comments about my mother made by mourners represent broadly held judgments—in this case ones intended to be salutary—that reflect widespread cultural views of what women should be.

The example is of my mother, yet hers is the story of a great many women. I recall and write about this as her daughter, yet I also approach this topic as one who has studied the larger issue of caring and its entrenched association with women. What I write, therefore, necessarily reflects both my experiences as her daughter and my knowledge and conclusions as someone who has examined extensively the ways in which our culture defines and limits women's roles and lives. I hope to weave my dual positions together to create a layered understanding that is both rich in human insight and sound in scholarship. Ideally, the two perspectives will complement one another so that my personal experiences enable me to illuminate human implications of existing theory and research, and my examination of broad sources of understanding provide a context that helps frame and inform specific events in my own life.

In this chapter, I look closely at one particular cultural definition of womanhood, suspending for the time being consideration of alternative images of women. Specifically, I examine what is involved in viewing selflessness and caring as the epitome of goodness in women such that the comments I overheard at my mother's funeral make sense as being consistent with and representative of widely held cultural views.

To do this, I examine structural features and social and discursive practices of our culture that foster the expectation that women should care for others. I then explore how these practices prepare women particularly well to meet the requirements implicit in the role of caregiver. In addition, I investigate the possible consequences of this role for the person giving care. Too infrequently have understandings of caregiving focused adequately on the ways in which this activity can burden and diminish those giving care. Thus, my analysis aims to understand the bases and implications of women's role as caregivers and how it has been constructed and practiced in the United States.

To launch this inquiry, I return to mother's story as exemplary of women who make caring for others the focus of their lives. I want to trace how her identity evolved from that of an independent, assertive individual to that of wife and mother. Understanding what transpired for her might provide clues about how similar transformations occur in the lives of many women.

After mother married, she worked while my father attended law school. Five years into the marriage the family consisted of my parents, my older sister, and myself. During this early chapter in our family's life mother continued working as a stockbroker. I remember many mornings when I watched her getting ready for work. There was an energy, a bounce to her movements as she dressed and coiffed her hair. In the evenings after work she seemed still full of energy as she fixed our dinners and spent time talking with my sister and me. I remember her as engaging and vibrant then.

Eight years after I entered the scene, mother became pregnant a third time, and my father decided it was time to move from Durham, North Carolina, to Roxboro, the small, friendly town in which he had grown up. At this point, my mother's firm dismissed her, explaining that she could not commute to work, a mere thirty miles each way, and be a "proper mother" to three young children. In the 1950s when this happened, there were no laws against sexist and discriminatory employment policies, so she had no recourse to this fiat decision by her employer. In Roxboro there were no professional opportunities for a woman, and my father dissuaded mother from taking the secretarial and clerical positions that were available since he considered these "unseemly" for the county attorney's wife. So in 1957 Carolyn was born and mother quit working.

In the years that followed, she showed constancy in taking care of my father, three, and eventually four, children, and our home. She became an expert seamstress and fashioned clothes that made us the envy of our classmates. She baked so frequently that our home more often than not was charmed by the yeasty smell of homemade breads. At first she spoke often and wistfully of her professional life and the excitement and sense of accomplishment it had provided. At first she still dressed stylishly and had energy for participating in, or at least tolerating with good humor, the usual adventures and misadventures of youngsters. Over time, however, she came to speak less of her former self, to recall with decreasing frequency "how I used to be," and eventually to state that being a homemaker was her choice, her preference. And over time she seemed to lose energy, as a balloon gradually loses its air, becoming a fatigued, deflated version of its once buoyant self.

Trying to understand that transformation now, I ask how could she have sealed off so much of who she was. Yet, almost immediately the converse question assaults me: how could she not have sealed off the identity she had crafted for herself if she was to live with any contentment in the world that others defined as appropriate for her?

Like many women of her time, she learned to accept restrictive, repressive social policies; and, again like other women, she coped by redefining the position the culture assigned as one chosen and preferred. This perhaps made it easier to abide the limits inherent in assigned roles and to find—or create—value within those constraints. Within the culturally prescribed roles for women, caring for others assumes particular prominence, so it may readily be seen as an appropriate and culturally condoned means of defining self and deriving self worth. All that one has to do is to forsake other possibilities for self and learn to put others' needs ahead of one's own.

While nothing about caring inherently restricts it to women, we cannot reasonably ignore the historical fact nor the continuing reality that women, more than men, have been expected to care for others. "Embedded in our notions of caring we see some of the deepest dimensions of traditional gender differentiation in our society," Tronto observes (1989). "Women care for their families, neighbors, and friends . . . by doing the concrete work of caring" (172). Because women have been so predominantly associated with giving care, my analysis focuses on caring as it is assigned to and enacted by women.[1]

In an insightful study of the association between women and caring in Western culture, Puka (1990) suggests that what happened in my mother's life is perhaps broadly representative of coping strategies that women use to survive in a sexist social order that severely limits their options. He argues that women must rationalize what is done to them and must see their position as "adult and self-chosen in its selectivity" in order to give themselves a sense they are "'taking control of one's life' and 'taking responsibility for oneself'" (62). Yet, Puka observes, women can do this only at the cost of the "self-alienation involved" (63). They must deny or repress their own interests to fit into the circumscribed role that is assigned by others and that women convince themselves is a personal choice.

The coping strategies that promote survival in oppressive circumstances are perhaps effective in allowing a person to be functional within the proscribed role, but they in no way lead to any critique, any challenge, of that role and its inherent constraints. The prerequisite for these coping strategies is a costly one: disowning whatever goals and self-conceptions one had that do not fit within it. Without the benefit of reading Puka's analysis, it seems my mother understood what she had to do in order to live the life allowed to her.

Her experience counseling women and couples allowed Jean Baker Miller (1976) to draw a critical insight about the process whereby women learn to find satisfaction in what the culture allows them to do: "Women have grown up knowing the goals most valued for individual development were not to be *their* goals. . . . Women have had to come up with a basis for worthiness that is different from that which the dominant culture bestows. They have effected enough of a creative internal transformation of values to allow themselves to believe that caring for people and participating in others' development is enhancing to self-esteem" (44–45). Even if not enhancing to self-esteem, we might add, caring for others may be the only culturally legitimated identity available to many women.

But we need to push Miller's statement further; she tells us there is a process of "creative internal transformation" but not how this process is actually brought off. If we can uncover the dynamics involved, then perhaps we can understand better how a person comes to regard self-worth as contingent on caring for others, often at the expense of caring for oneself. To do this, we first need to clarify what is meant by caring; then we may proceed to consider what kinds of attitudes, feelings, and activities are associated with caring and what the costs of such engagement may be.

Defining Care

Most scholars and practitioners concerned with care agree that it is an extremely difficult term to define and one for which meanings are diverse. Some writers focus on caring as an activity. Finch and Groves (1983), for instance, call it a "labor of love." Others focus on the attitudes or orientations that give rise to caring activities. Prominent in this group are Sara Ruddick (1980, 1989), who has done much to illuminate the kinds of thinking involved in care giving, and Carol Gilligan (1982), who has theorized the ethical orientations underlying the tendency to care. Clearly, caring includes both particular practices or activities and the kinds of thinking, attitudes, and moral stances that motivate one to care. In this book, I assume both concrete activities and underlying motivations are entailed in caring.

This still leaves us with the question of what precisely caring is. In an insightful analysis, Joan Tronto (1989) distinguishes between two basic kinds of caring. *Caring about*, Tronto defines as concern with rather abstract phenomena; for example, one may care about security, money, values, the country. *Caring for*, by contrast, "implies a specific, particular object that is the focus of caring. . . . Caring for involves responding to the particular, concrete, physical, spiritual, intellectual, psychic, and emotional needs of others," a kind of activity Tronto notes is closely and specifically associated with women in Western culture (174–175). It should be clear that my interest lies in caring for, rather than caring about. Since women disproportionately engage in caring for in Western culture, their activities command my primary attention; however, I neither assume nor mean to imply that only women care for others.

My focus on concrete, particular activities that comprise caring for another person does not reflect any assumption that caring is or must be confined to the private sphere of personal relationships. My position, for instance, is wholly distinct from that of Nel Noddings (1984), who argues that genuine caring can occur only in personal relationships. My focus is an analytic choice designed to limit what I discuss, but this does not imply either that I regard caring as exclusively within the private domain or that I think what happens in close personal relationships is unrelated to the larger culture within which they exist. Clearly, how we conduct our private lives and how we constitute our public world exist in a dialectical relationship: what we do in our close associations reflects understandings of appropriate roles and conduct that are derived from prevailing views in the larger culture; conversely, the ideals and assumptions that comprise public life are constituted, in part, by individual acts whose genesis is often in private relationships. At a later point I will elaborate this, arguing that much of what is currently going on in the private sphere provides an impetus for reforming broad cultural definitions of women and care.

Cultural Definitions of Caring for Others

We want now to consider what our culture defines, however implicitly, as the qualities needed to be a good caregiver. In other words, we are asking what kinds of qualities, abilities, and ways of thinking people associate with caring for others and, by implication, expect of someone who is responsible for providing care. Studies in a number of disciplines recurringly identify three qualities as particularly prominent in people who care for others; relatedly, these same qualities consistently surface in expectations of caregivers: partiality, empathy, and a willingness to serve or nurture others. It's impossible to discern whether enactment of these qualities is a response to expectations or whether expectations have grown out of concrete practices of care, or both. We do know, however, that these three qualities are closely associated with caring for others.

Partiality

In the 1800s, Hegel argued that women's presence in politics jeopardizes the state because "women regulate their actions not by the demands of universality, but by arbitrary inclinations and opinions" (263–264). This very same particularistic altruism that disqualifies women for public citizenship, Hegel claimed, was required of them if they were to be suited to the role of wife and mother, which calls upon women to be especially motivated by feelings for the members of her family. That view of women and their inclinations retains substantial support nearly two centuries after Hegel penned it.

Hegel, then, tells us that partiality is a vice for public activities but a virtue in the private sphere where women are expected, indeed perhaps required, to be very partial to those whose care is entrusted to them. Partiality and its contrasting concept, impartiality, lie at the heart of conventional moral theory; more important perhaps, acting partially or impartially is often understood within our culture as evidence of caring or not caring. We need to understand both terms if we are to appreciate the role partiality occupies in cultural understandings of what it means to care for others.

For Kohlberg, arguably the leading theorist of moral development in this century, impartiality is essential to moral maturity. Beginning with his dissertation in 1958, Kohlberg based his research on the concrete practices of thought and action he observed in males as they developed over time. Grounding theory in human behavior continued to characterize Kohlberg's work (1981, 1984), so his theory offers us an explanation of how men actually conceive and practice morality. To be a truly moral agent, Kohlberg insists, one must act on the basis of *universality*, which is to say one must act impartially toward all others in the same manner; specifically, one must not show partiality in favoring one person over another, for to do so is to transgress the conventional moral imperative to be fair.[2]

Inquiring further into the principle of universality, we find impartially toward all others requires viewing them from a vantage point removed from concrete individuals and situations (Kant, 1965). The impartial view is an abstracted one that theoretically incorporates the perspectives of all others into a single gestalt viewpoint designed to provide equal fairness and good for everyone (Kant, 1965; Rawls, 1971). Judgments from this abstracted position, it is assumed, need not take into account the particular needs, wants, and interests of unique others, since the generalized perspective includes automatically all individuals (Unger, 1975; for a critique, see Bordo, 1987).

By contrast, to be partial is to focus quite directly on the concrete perspectives, needs, concerns, and the like of particular others. It requires a person to "view each and every rational being as an individual with a concrete history, identity and affective-emotional constitution" (Benhabib, 1987, 87) and to act toward an other on that basis, rather than on some abstracted conception of what all people are like and what all people are entitled to receive. A person acting in accord with a principle of partiality, thus, sees herself or himself as thoroughly embedded in the complex world of relationships, personalities, and contexts and recognizes those toward whom s/he acts as similarly encumbered by particular personal, interpersonal, and cultural circumstances. This stance informs efforts to recognize and meet the unique needs and desires of particular persons, rather than to act on abstract and general ideas about what people need.

Another distinction between partial and impartial actions concerns the extent of emotion or feeling involved. The principle of universality and its related emphasis on impartial behavior requires "being dispassionate: being entirely unaffected by feelings in one's judgment. . . . Only by expelling desire, affectivity and the body from reason can impartiality achieve its unity" (Young, 1987, 62). Reflective of the Western division of reason and emotion, this viewpoint holds that feeling would compromise—indeed, preclude—rational judgment.[3] In short, impartiality requires one to be disinterested in others and situations toward which one acts.

By contrast, partiality—the inclination associated with caring and, not coincidentally, with women—requires just the opposite: that one be affected by feelings, especially those toward others for whom one cares. In her analysis of human development, Chodorow (1978) calls attention to partiality as a criterion distinguishing women from men: "Women's role in the home and primary definition in social reproductive, sex-gender terms are characterized by particularism, concern with affective goals and ties" while "men's primary definition in the sphere of production [is] universalistically defined and . . . less likely to involve affective considerations" (180). Caring, so closely associated with and expected of women, then, directly necessitates feelings for others whom one views with deliberate favoritism. Kohlberg (1984) agrees that care relationships require partiality; he argues, however, such relationships lie outside the realm of morality for which impartiality and universality remain the essential principles.

To be caring, then, one must be partial, which Benhabib (1987) suggests involves thinking and acting in ways that are "more contextual, more immersed in the details of relationships and narratives . . . [and demonstrating] a greater propensity to take the standpoint of the 'particular other' [that] women appear more adept at" (78). Our understandings of care assume it will involve partiality; we expect caregivers to regard others in very particularistic ways and act toward them with feeling for their unique nature, needs, and circumstances. It is this idea of acting with feeling that provides a bridge to a second cultural understanding of what caring involves.

Empathy

In order to care well, it is necessary to have empathy—insight into others' perspectives, feelings, and needs. Empathizing with others is essential to providing care that is responsive to their particular needs and wants. Elaborating this idea, Blum (1988) notes that it is "informed by care, love, empathy, compassion, and emotional sensitivity" (475) in which "emotion, cognition and action [are] not readily separable. Knowing what to do involves knowing others and being connected in ways involving both emotion and cognition" (476). The affective aspect of this is the feeling for another, the wish to understand and assist; yet this alone is not enough. Also necessary is the cognitive ability to gain and understand what another needs. In turn, as Tronto (1989) points out, such knowledge requires that "the caring person must devote much attention to learning what the other person might need" (177).

To understand why women have been both more expected and more likely to exhibit empathy, we need to make an excursion into psychoanalytic theory. Insight into the socialization and development characteristic of women comes primarily from two major works, Jean Baker Miller's *Toward a New Psychology of Women* (1976; rev. 1986) and Nancy Chodorow's *Reproduction of Mothering* (1978), and has been elaborated and applied by a host of others (for example, Dinnerstein, 1976; Flax, 1978; Gilligan, 1982; Mitchell, 1975; Rubin, 1985). Importantly, all of these studies are based primarily on observations and analyses of people acting in their real-life situations and offering their own descriptions of what they do and how they feel in those instances. According to Chodorow, as well as others working out of her theories, female children tend to develop within relationships with others, especially the primary parent, who is typically the mother. Chodorow notes that high levels of identification "are particularly characteristic of early relationships between mothers and daughters" (104), a psychodynamic that shapes the feminine sense of identity in its most formative stage. From the start, female infants are kept physically and psychologically closer than are male infants. This enforced relatedness is elaborated by the likeness between a female infant and the mother: a daughter, unlike a son, can define her identity within the relationship with her mother. She is like the mother and need not differentiate radically from her in order to form an initial sense of herself. Thus, from the start, females learn to make connections with others and to define themselves within relationships rather than independent of others.

This process, known as gender identification, occurs concurrently with the second major developmental task, which is to establish ego boundaries. To do this, a child must recognize where he or she stops and others begin—a distinction between self and others. Yet, the means of doing this tend to differ markedly for the two sexes. Encouraged from birth to understand themselves and their own identities within the relationship with mother, female infants tend to establish permeable ego boundaries. The line between self and other is tenuous, never solid or sealed. Chodorow's clinical observations led her to theorize that the female child's intense and prolonged early identification with her mother leads the child to draw a line that is necessarily blurred not only with the mother, the original source of identification, but with people in general. In short, argues Chodorow, through the early relationship with the mother—specifically the identification between mother and daughter—the young girl comes to know herself, to understand herself as not really separate from others but as interconnected with them (166). Not limited to childhood, this sense of being interdependent with others forms a key foundation of the sense of self throughout life. One consequence especially pertinent to women's tendency to care for others is in experiencing others as intertwined with themselves; females often sense others' feelings, to a degree, as their own. Males generally erect more rigid ego boundaries that demarcate a clear line between themselves and others. Consequently, males who have been socialized as most males are in

Western culture are not likely to be able to conceive fully what
another thinks or feels, much less to experience another's feelings
and thoughts as their own. In general, boys learn to define themselves as independent of others, an orientation that carries into
adulthood when men typically maintain distance—a firm line
between themselves and others—even in their close relationships.
Chodorow's summary of differences in developmental processes characteristic of females and males merits lengthy quo-
tation:

> Girls emerge [from the early developmental process] . . .
> with a basis for "empathy" built into their primary definition
> of self in a way that boys do not. Girls emerge with a stronger
> basis for experiencing another's needs or feelings as one's
> own. . . . [By contrast,] boys come to define themselves as
> more separate and distinct with a greater sense of rigid ego
> boundaries and differentiation. The basic feminine sense
> of self is connected to the world, the basic masculine sense
> of self is separate. . . . Masculine personality, then, comes
> to be defined more in terms of denial of relation and connec-
> tion . . . , whereas feminine personality comes to include a
> fundamental definition of self in relationship. Thus, rela-
> tional abilities and preoccupations have been extended in
> women's development and curtailed in men's. (167, 169)

It is important to realize that studies of female development
do not suggest the ability to take the perspective of others is
always, or even typically, consciously controlled. Rather, it is
regarded as a predictable consequence for anyone socialized
within relationships and whose identity from birth is mapped in
relation to others. Thus, the capacity to understand another's
thoughts and feelings seems not to result from choice, instinct,
or biological capability but rather from particular kinds of socialization during the formative period of infancy.
    Speaking to this point, Chodorow insists that "feminine per-
sonality comes to define itself in relation and connection to other
people more than masculine personality" (1974, 43–44), because
females experience themselves "as more continuous with and
related to" others (1978, 167). Elaborating this, clinicians Eichenbaum and Orbach (1983a) claim that "women's psychology is
one of unclear boundaries. . . . The central aspect of women's

psychology, the one that embodies most of the major themes, is the lack of psychological separateness" (138). "By contrast," writes Chodorow (1990), "men develop a self based more on denial of relation and on a more fixed, firmly split, and repressed inner self-object world" (119).

Empathy, then, seems best understood as a quality learned in the process of acquiring what Chodorow (1990) calls a "relational self" (121), which is typically associated with females and traced to early experiences in families. The typicality here refers to the result of standard patterns of socialization in Western culture which predispose females to define themselves more relationally than males do. Chodorow (1978, 1990), it should be noted, is unambiguous in rejecting biological explanations of the relational self in favor of psychoanalytic ones that emphasize family experiences. That the relational self is formed by specific, identifiable psychological processes is underscored by Hartsock's (1983) observation that "the material conditions of women's lives produce in women an experience of self in relation to others . . . and a sense of variety of connectedness with other persons" (242).

The developmental pattern characteristic of females accounts for empathy and, relatedly, tendencies to attend to particular others in partial ways and to internalize others' feelings—perhaps, in fact, to be unable not to feel what others do. In turn, this complex of qualities sheds light on a third aspect of caring for others: willingness to serve or nurture others.

Willingness to Serve or Nurture Others

A tendency to nurture others emanates naturally out of inclinations to see others in unique, individual ways and to experience their thoughts and feelings in a manner somewhere between experience that is direct and that which is entirely removed from oneself. Nurturance, enacted through efforts to enhance others' growth and/or comfort, in fact, seems contingent on being able to recognize another's particular nature and needs (partiality) and being affectively aware of another's feelings, thoughts, and needs (empathy).

Speaking to this point, Miller (1976) observes that "women have traditionally built a sense of self-worth on activities that they can manage to define as taking care of and giving to others" (54). In a subsequent expansion of this idea, Miller states more strongly that "the organization of one's life around serving others is such a central factor for women that . . . it can be seen as an overriding [theme]. . . . [W]omen have been led to feel that they can integrate and use all their attributes if they use them for others . . . to attune themselves to the wishes, desires, and needs of others" (61–62). Thus, writing in 1986, Miller repeats the message *Life* broadcast three decades earlier: women can and should use their capacities to take care of others.

Gilligan (1982) theorizes that the capacity to care responsively for very specific others evolves through three levels. Since, however, her analysis demonstrates neither a sequential progression among the "levels" nor a tendency not to regress to what she labels less mature levels, these are better conceived as types or kinds of caring, which are not necessarily sequentially related (see Puka, 1990, 61). Each of the types of caring Gilligan identifies pivots centrally on an understanding that self and others are connected.

In the first type of caring, the inclination to care is experienced primarily as a wish to protect the self from more powerful others; to do this, the self must learn to read others and to respond in ways that keep them satisfied and unaggressive toward the self (75–77, 110, and following). This orientation differs from a second type of caring that focuses on conventional social views of "goodness," notably exercising tact, not hurting others, and winning the approval of others by identifying and serving their needs and desires (66–78)—what Puka (1990) has labeled a "service orientation" (61). The third type, which Gilligan defines as the height of moral maturity in women, attempts to balance nurturing others and caring for self so that persons are honored.

Moral maturity, Gilligan argues, uniquely reflects the strength of caring and, by association, women's ways of relating to others. She represents this as a powerful position because in it one recognizes both the desire in oneself to be responsive to others (to some degree) and the latitude of freedom one has within others' expectations. For Gilligan, the distinction between the second and third kinds of caring seems to lie in the degree to which a woman reflects on the constraints confronting her. Unlike the uncritical acceptance of the service orientation in type-two caring, in type-three a woman recognizes others' power and the ways in which it constrains her, and she opts to restrict her own initiatives of strength and self-interest to those areas "allowed" by others, including ones the society in general defines as appropriate.

What a person enacting this third kind of care may not recognize is the extent to which she must not see, not know certain longings and self-interests in order to maintain her position in a context that rather narrowly circumscribes choices. Further, a person at this "level of moral maturity" does not question the bases of the desire to serve that she has carried forward; the injunction to serve others is accepted as a given as is the closely bounded margin of freedom that remains open. In short, attention appears to focus more on enjoying what one can have than on realizing what one cannot have.

Acceptance of the premise that one should be of service to others, combined with the socialized capacities to see others as individuals and to understand their feelings, comprise what is generally expected of a person who cares for others. In tandem, these three qualities invite a strong focus on others, both to understand their needs and to discern what limited freedom remains for the self. In Miller's (1986) opinion, "Women's reality *is* rooted in the encouragement to 'form' themselves into the person who will be of benefit to others" (73).

This analysis of what caregiving entails and how the expected qualities are rather systematically inculcated into females sheds light on the "creative transformation" that many women make in order to function within the roles assigned to them. It also illuminates the process by which my mother reformed herself from the person she had created in the first thirty years of her life into one who could survive in the circumstances permitted her during her remaining thirty-eight years. It reveals why the only reasonable question to pose is not How could she have repressed so much of herself? but rather How could she not have abandoned her strong, self-created identity and still functioned in the radically circumscribed situation in which she found herself? She had to give up and, eventually, deny that former self to live the only life that was possible for her.

In summary, caring seems to entail (at least) partiality, empathy, and a willingness to serve or nurture others. This understanding of caregiving and how it is cultivated particularly in

women positions us to pursue a companion question that is less ·
frequently addressed: what are the consequences or costs of this
caregiving orientation for the individual who demonstrates care?
Perhaps this concern is better phrased as one in which we attempt
to identify the potential dangers for someone who cares for
others, since the frequency of their manifestation should not be
conflated with necessary or causal relationships. Even while we
recognize these consequences as less than necessary, however,
the extent to which they do in fact occur should not be minimized.

The Potential Costs of Caring

Concern about the consequences women often suffer for their
tendencies to care was a theme in an early paper by Barbara
Houston (1985) in which she wrote, "When I reflect on the history
of women, I realize how much our caring has nurtured and
empowered others. I see how good it has been for others. However, I also see how terribly costly it has been for women. And
so the first question for me is . . . can an ethics of care avoid self-
sacrifice?" (7).

Houston is not alone in questioning what caring costs women.
Rhode (1990a, 6) points out that the cultural tendency has been
to extol women's tendency to care, entirely predictable since this
serves the purposes of those who generally benefit from women's
care. Caring for others has even been defined as power since
care relationships are necessarily asymmetrical ones in which the
person giving care has power over the other. Yet, as Schweickart
(1990) incisively observes, "Although power is distributed in favor of the one caring, it is exercised in the service of the cared for"
(91). And serving others is generally assigned to and expected
predominantly of women, a fact that led Miller to title a chapter
in her book "Serving Others' Needs—Doing for Others" and to
state in that chapter's opening paragraph that "serving others is
a basic principle around which women's lives are organized; it
is far from such for men" (61).

It thus becomes important to inquire more carefully into the
ways in which caring can be costly for caregivers. Three broad
and closely interrelated costs are regularly mentioned by individuals who provide care. Corroborating these self-reports are observations from those who study and work with people involved

in caregiving in which the same three effects figure prominently. The apparently most typical costs are motivational displacement, compromised or undeveloped autonomy, and low status.

Motivational Displacement

Although caring is thought of in terms of feeling, as we've already seen, it also requires the cognitive capacity to gain, comprehend, and make inferences from knowledge of the one cared for. The cognitive dimensions of caring have been of interest to those studying the actual ways in which people exercise care. Knowledge of another's perspective is clearly one cognitive aspect of caring.

Another cognitive aspect of caring has been identified by clinicians who observe people involved in care relationships. Nel Noddings insists that the key cognitive dimension of caring is motivational displacement. This involves displacing one's own interests and motives for those of the person for whom one cares. "Our mental engrossment is on the cared-for, not on ourselves," Noddings notes (1984, 24). Continuing this discussion, Noddings uses herself as an example: "My motive energy flows toward the other and perhaps, though not necessarily towards his ends. . . . I allow my motive energy to be shared; I put it at the service of the other" (33). Motivational displacement, then, occurs when a person's motives for acting are centered on someone other than the self—the other takes prominence, and it is within the perspective of the other that a caregiver organizes her (or his) own goals, thoughts, and feelings.

One indicator of motivational displacement is preoccupation with giving, a demonstrably more pronounced issue for women than for men. Drawing on her psychotherapeutic experiences, Miller (1986) reports that "women often spend a great deal more time talking about giving than men do. Women constantly confront themselves with questions about giving. Am I giving enough? Can I give enough? Why don't I give enough? . . . They are upset if they feel they are not givers" (50). Preoccupation with giving reflects an intense focus on what others want, need, and expect; it is, in short, a process of thinking of one's own actions in terms of others' motives, expectations, and judgments.

To do this it is necessary to displace—or misplace or deny—one's own motives, which might conflict with those of others. When preoccupation with others is chronic, as in the case of women whose lives center on caring for their families, eventually a person may not have to exert much energy to displace her own motives: they have been silenced effectively. The caregiver comes not just to be defined by others but to define herself in their terms, according to their motives, from their perspectives. Miller (1986) cites a recurrent example of this from her clinical practice: "As wives, mothers, daughters, lovers, or workers, women often feel that other people are demanding too much of them; and they resent it. Frequently they cannot even allow themselves to admit that they resent these excess pressures. They have come to believe that they should *want* to respond at all times and in all ways" (51). At this point the displacement of one's own motives by those of others is complete.

Motivational displacement deeply affects the individual experiencing it. It raises concerns about the very loss of self since, as Tronto (1989) notes, what is required is nothing short of "losing one's own concerns in order to see clearly the concerns of the cared-for" (178). The grave danger is that the caregiver may become an object to herself, much as she is an object to others, who see her in terms of her capacity to meet their needs and enhance their comfort. Again, Miller is instructive: "When one is an object, not a subject, all of one's own physical and sexual impulses and interests are presumed not to exist independently. They are to be brought into existence only by and for others—controlled, defined, and used" (60). Even Noddings (1984), a strong advocate of caring for others, recognizes "the danger is that caring . . . requires a constitutive engrossment and displacement of motivation" (25).

In her incisive analysis of women's roles in the United States, Elizabeth Janeway (1971) describes not professional caregivers or women who seek counseling, but the average wife and mother whose life is arranged by, around, and for others. She reports that a woman is "subject to call by other people and often at the convenience of other people. . . . She must be ready to respond . . . when it is needed by the other member or members of a relationship and so she stands by, waiting to be called on, but not the initiator of action. In this situation she doesn't make decisions, she accepts them from others" (86). Little wonder, then, Janeway concludes that women's traditional role directs them "toward responsiveness rather than decisiveness" (87).

Preoccupation with giving and the larger tendency to displace one's own motives have the potential to induce caregivers to deny, distort, devalue, or otherwise repress their own impulses, goals, needs, and desires. Carried to its logical culmination this repression can lead one to define basic identity in terms of others or—put more precisely—in the terms *of* others.

More extensively probing women's tendency to think in terms of others, Eichenbaum and Orbach (1987) observe that a woman "begins to identify the satisfying of others' needs and complying with others as a *need of her own*" (61). At this point a caregiver can no longer distinguish what others want or need from what she wants and needs. This displacement of motives and, eventually, of personal identity is reflected in the frequently made claim of caregivers: I am serving (or giving to) myself by serving (or giving to) others. Self and others' motives are so thoroughly intertwined that they are synonymous: self's motives have become those of the others. Defining one's self in terms of others leads to a second potential cost of caregiving.

Compromised or Undeveloped Autonomy

Eschewing a simplistic indictment of women's tendencies to be connected to and caring of others, Chodorow (1990) nonetheless recognizes caregiving's potential to diminish autonomy. A "woman's relational self can be a strength or a pitfall in feminine psychic life; it enables empathy, nurturance, and intimacy but threatens to undermine autonomy and to dissolve self into others" (121). Taking a more pointed stance, Rhode (1990a) argues that "women's disproportionate assumption of caretaking responsibilities has encouraged forms of psychological dependence . . . that carry heavy costs. That this 'down side' of difference has received inadequate attention should not be surprising" (6), by which Rhode means that those who wield power in our culture are well served by not noticing what caregiving costs women.

What does it mean to compromise or dilute an autonomous sense of identity? It implies quite simply that a person does not see or think of self apart from others. More than recognizing the ways in which one is connected to others, loss of autonomy involves not being able to see ways in which one is not related to others. A person comes to understand and think of herself through others, in relationship to others, as defined by others such that she loses—or, in some cases, never has the opportunity to develop—any independent conception of selfhood. This leads almost inevitably to substantial dependence on others to confer self-worth and to define one's own identity.

Pointing out the danger of losing a sense of who one is does not require us to embrace a static conception of autonomy as rigidly separated from others. Clearly, this would seriously jeopardize caring and might additionally restrict selfhood in the converse respect of losing awareness of interdependence. Instead, it seems more reasonable to suggest the prudence of a fluid, dynamic conception of autonomy in which an individual recognizes both self and others, acknowledges both that relationships are important to one's identity and that self chosen, individual activities that are worthy of pursuit (Keller, 1985). When autonomy is severely compromised, however, any sense of identity beyond relationships with others can be lost, no longer visible to oneself or others. One ceases to be the "captain of my ship" or the "master of my soul." Instead, one becomes a passenger on others' ships, an observer rather than a creator of her own soul.

The motivational displacement that is promoted by caring for others encourages caregivers to conceive their own actions, attitudes, and values only as these are mediated through and defined by others. In turn, for the caregiver, "mediation is not directly with reality but with and through *the other person's purposes* in that reality," reflecting a selfhood that hinges "ultimately on the other person's perceptions and evaluations, rather than one's own" (Miller, 1986, 73). In fact, this may be an understatement in suggesting some option between an other's perceptions and one's own; for the person whose motives are constantly and thoroughly displaced in another, there may not be any secure basis for perceiving and evaluating self outside of others' perspectives. In short, one may lose one's own terms.

Elaborating this process and its relationship to motivational displacement, Miller (1986) explains that in Western culture "women are encouraged to do two things. First, they are diverted from exploring and expressing their needs. . . . Secondly, women are encouraged to 'transform' their own needs. This often means they fail, *automatically and without perceiving it*, to recognize their own needs as such. They come to see their needs as if they were identical to those of others—usually men and children" (19, emphasis added). Particularly noteworthy is Miller's insight that this "transformation" is typically not conscious. In fact, for the process to work it *must be* less than conscious, for if one fully apprehended it, resistance or dissonance would ensue.

How does this explanation of loss of an autonomous self fit into my mother's story? Perhaps as she displaced her own motives with those of my father and us children and came to see herself in our terms, she actually didn't realize—didn't let herself know—that we and she were colluding to supplant her self-created identity with one that better served our purposes.

Yet, I wonder whether that transformation always stayed comfortably beneath her consciousness. During the time mother lived with us, a revealing incident occurred. When I arrived home late one time after an evening committee meeting on campus, Mom informed me one of my students had called. "I answered," she told me, "and the student said, 'Oh, you must be Dr. Wood's mother.'" Then, in a moment of rare self-reflexiveness Mother said, "Funny, for forty years I was Charles's wife and now I'm your mother. I used to be myself." When I asked her to tell me more about what that meant to her, the defenses were quickly locked back into place with a laugh and a dismissive, "But this is how I wanted it after all." To which "I" was she referring as wanting that identity?

Transformation of identity is usually effected so gradually that the adoption of another's perspective as one's own is outside of the realm of awareness and, therefore, beyond reflection, much less challenge.[4] Were this not the case, a person would be likely to experience constant and severe dissonance in recognizing the discrepancy between her selves and her lives. Yet, not being conscious of something is not the same as not suffering from it. There are costs in repressing one's self-chosen identity and living out others' definitions of yourself. Dorothy Smith (1987) points out that women's roles as caregivers require "a subordination of attentiveness to self and a focus on others, the lack of development of an independent project . . . and, in contrast, an openness and attentiveness to cues and indications of others' needs" (66).

Because a self with its own motives, projects, and interests interferes with attentiveness to others, caregivers are induced to displace any autonomous sense of self.

Janeway (1971) sharply reminds us that "vicarious living, which means acting and feeling through others, should not be confused with living in affection and community *with* others" (177). The person who has lost her sense of autonomy is condemned to live a life one perspective removed from itself, a life both constrained and made possible by that very distance. And this kind of life is a predictable, logical outcome of socialization that trains a person to tune into others' needs, desires, feelings and to place those needs ahead of one's own.

Motivational displacement and diminishment of autonomy are substantial potential costs of caregiving, yet they are not the only ones. Compounding these losses is a third cost: devaluation of what one is required or, at the very least, expected to do and be. Our culture creates a double bind for women by expecting and training them to be concerned with caring for others while steadfastly refusing to recognize or reward them for it.

The Social Construction of Caregiving: Devalued and Low Status

"When we can only think in terms given by the dominant culture," Miller (1986) cautions, referring to what happens when motivational displacement and loss of autonomy occur, "and when that culture does not attend to our own experiences but specifically denies and devalues them, we are left with no way of conceptualizing our lives" (58). This illuminates a third serious cost of giving care: Western culture does not routinely acknowledge, much less value, caregiving. Instead, it regards caring for others as something that certain people are expected or required to do but for which they will not be recognized or rewarded in substantial ways.

What Western culture does value is individual achievement. The dominant cultural ethos champions the individual who shows ambition, pursues self-interests, accomplishes things, and in general operates independently of others. This pervasive cultural ideal contrasts strongly with the cultural view of women and what they should do and be. Karlyn Campbell (1973) points this out in an early essay when she observes that "the sex role requirements for women contradict the dominant values of American culture—self-reliance, achievement, independence" (75). This insight recurs in Rosenblum's (1989) more recent analysis of the conflict between the overall ideals of Western culture and its definitions of femininity: "While the culture stresses individuation and self promotion, femininity encourages one to self-sacrifice and subordinate" (199). The incompatibility between ideals of women and cultural ideals for individuals has been noted by many other scholars (for example, Broverman, 1970; Horner, 1971; Ruble, 1983) including Janeway (1971), who declares, "Woman's role puts her at odds not only with the American ethos, but with the whole long trend of Western civilization toward individual freedom and individual responsibility . . . woman's traditional role *in itself* is opposed to a deeply significant aspect of our culture" (99).

This discrepancy between the requirements for femininity and the cultural ethos is compounded by the culture's simultaneous disregard for what it expects, or require, of women: caring. "In our culture," Miller (1976) notes, "'serving others' is for losers, it is low-level stuff. Yet serving others is the basic principle around which women's lives are organized" (61). Continuing this line of thought, Miller argues, "The large element of human activity that involves doing for others has been separated off and assigned to women. [And] . . . this is combined with the fact that what women do is generally not recognized" (70; also see Cornell, 1991; Polatnick, 1973).

Integrating these ideas, it becomes clear that women are expected to engage in activities that the culture does not value; thus, they are required, or at the very least strongly encouraged, to be persons the culture does not value. Inevitably this creates a paradox in which a woman cannot win. If she acts in accord with the dominant values of the culture, she will be faulted for not being a "good woman," for being "unnatural," for being hard and uncaring; if, instead, she follows the cultural dictates for being a good woman, she risks being devalued by the culture and, quite possibly, by herself since she is not immune to cultural views of women and caring (Wood & Conrad, 1983). In effect, this forces those devoted to caring for others to realize, on the one hand, that their culture doesn't really value what they do and, on the other hand, that the culture firmly expects them to do it. Obviously it's difficult, if not impossible, to feel good about oneself when one is "assigned a role which is somehow at odds with the ideals of the common culture" (Janeway, 1971, 99–100). It is highly unlikely that the predominance of women in caregiving roles is coincidental. It is more understandable as the "logical," almost inevitable outcome of growing up in a society that teaches women to look to others for support, approval, and definition. As a direct result of this, Miller (1986) claims, "The characteristics most highly developed in women . . . are *the* very characteristics that are specifically dysfunctional for success in the world as it is" (124). The cycle continues: because women are socialized to act in ways discordant with the cultural ethos, women may well not fit comfortably into the mainstream of public life; because they don't fit well or excel there, they focus their primary energies in the sphere where they do fit—domestic life and relationships—and, thus, reinforce the assumptions of what a woman is and is not.

Socialized within relationships and taught from the earliest age to attend to others, women are systematically prepared for caregiving roles. Performing these roles allows women to gain approval and preserve relationships with others, while at the same time it deprives them of substantial personal freedom, status, and recognition in their culture.

Socialization, particularly during the formative early years, establishes principles for defining self-worth and satisfaction that tend to remain major influences throughout life. In an interesting study of women's perceptions of success and satisfaction, Markus (1987) reports that among her participants "even when women entered the public sphere of economy as, in principle, the equals of male breadwinners, for the majority of them success remained defined not through 'external' criteria of career achievement, but in terms of personal experience interpreted as satisfaction. At the same time, this feeling of satisfaction was often derived from the character and quality of interpersonal contacts, from the ability to be 'useful' to others, to take care and to help" (101). This orientation toward success, it should be noted, may account in large part for the disproportionate segregation of women into careers and positions with low status and compensation (Barrett, 1980; Barron & Norris, 1976).

In analyzing women's tendencies to focus on relationships even in the public sphere of work and politics, it is exceedingly difficult to separate informed choice for particular values from a learned inclination to value certain activities because those are what one is "supposed" to do. Some feminist theorists argue for the legitimacy of women's orientations toward work and, more generally, life, claiming that they are life affirming, life enhancing, and professionally appropriate: they insist that women's deviation from established and, de facto male, standards for success and professionalism represents not an inability, but an unwillingness to follow the male pattern. They advocate changing the terms of work to incorporate women's concerns and values rather than accepting the terms that have historically prevailed (Friedan, 1981; Gilligan, 1982; Markus, 1987).

Others, however, view women's difference as deviance that results either from innate or socialized abilities and inabilities of women. Either way, they claim, attitudes and tendencies conventionally associated with women are out of place in the public sphere. For women who want to "make it" in public life, the advice is to learn to "play the game," the game, that is, as it already exists and has existed since industrialization began (Helmich, 1974; Powell & Butterfield, 1981; Schein, 1975; Schwartz, 1989).

The genesis of generalizable differences in men's and women's orientations to success is an issue to which I return in chapter 4. A separate issue that merits more immediate attention is how these differences are evaluated—what meaning is attached to them. In Western culture an orientation that prioritizes helping others, sustaining relationships, and showing care is not widely acknowledged, much less valued beyond the level of lip service; an orientation that emphasizes advancing self, acting autonomously, and abiding by rules of fairness is revered, is, in fact, elevated to a cultural ideal. As Rosenblum (1989) concludes in her analysis of current cultural definitions of the sexes, "While the tenets of femininity encourage women to sacrifice for others, the cultural values provide little external validation or reward for that sacrifice" (200). An important implication of this is that caregiving is a culturally devalued activity and one for which women are systematically prepared and to which they are systematically assigned both by cultural forces and their own expectations as persons who have internalized the dictates of their social order.

Coming full circle now, we can pull together the issues examined in this chapter. We began by observing the widely held cultural equation between being a "good woman" and caring for others. This equation led us to inquire into the kinds of skills, attitudes, and personal orientations that people in our society assume should be present in someone who cares for others, and we found that partiality, empathy, and willingness to serve others are prominently associated with effective caring. These very qualities are ones that are emphasized in the socialization of women, but not men, a fact that illuminates the strong empirical association between women and caring. In large part, that association seems to arise out of women's historical embeddedness in relationships with others and, specifically, in caring for others. Particular practices of socialization that teach women to be sensitive and responsive to others uniquely prepare them to continue occupying this place within cultural life.

Considering the potential consequences of caring in Western culture enables us to understand better how this activity and the orientation underlying it frequently affects caregivers. Attending to others promotes motivational displacement, which can lead a caregiver to think predominantly in terms of the other and in the other's terms, eventually perhaps forgetting any terms of her own. In turn, motivational displacement promotes diminished autonomy as the caregiver increasingly comes to think of herself as an object, an object whose purpose is to serve others. Finally, we saw that the role of caregiver invites not only personal losses of individual motives and autonomy but also social losses in terms of status, prestige, respect, and material rewards.

In a culture that prizes independent action and achievement, the caregiver is marked as low level, low status. While these three dangers may not always result from caring for others, they are clearly invited by the requirements of caring itself. Requiring a focus on others and their needs and an ability to know and feel for others creates a compelling basis for losses of individual motivation, autonomy, and status.

The cultural devaluation is sometimes labeled the culture's problem, its misjudgment or misplacement of priorities (Gilligan, 1982). Yet as long as our culture continues to devalue caring, it is the caregiver who suffers the consequences of that problem. In this case, the public becomes the personal. To argue that people should care for others simply because to do so is "good" or "right" overlooks the critical point that good and right are not empirical phenomena, but ideals created through the discursive practices of a culture. Our culture has not, in fact, defined caring for others as important or worthy or even as good and right— except for some people who are also and not coincidentally defined and located in the margins of the culture. Until and unless we change how our culture construes caring, it is unrealistic to expect those who are assigned to do it to have high self-esteem and clear, personally fashioned identities. It is similarly unrealistic to expect individuals to choose consciously an identity and set of activities that will clearly not result in influence, status, respect, or security.

What I could not comprehend as my mother's daughter I can better understand from the reports and insights of those who have studied how caring actually works and what it means in our culture. The analysis in this chapter clarifies the process by which my mother, like anyone with a self-created identity, could gradually transform herself into Charles's wife and Dr. Wood's mother. It also helps us realize why this transformation perhaps has to be largely unconscious and unadmitted. By disowning her former self and claiming the identity conferred by society and her family as her own choice, my mother was able to preserve a coherent, integrated sense of herself and was able to be effective in the role assigned to her—she was a "good woman." Not acknowledging this transformation doubtlessly made it more comfortable to live with the life and identity that was feasible for her in her circumstances.

Keeping in mind what this examination has revealed about how Western culture defines caring and what costs potentially inhere in the practice of it, we turn next to an analysis of one particular text that has been highly influential in reinvigorating beliefs that women are and should be caring. We want to understand this book as both an argument in its own right and as a part of the larger, ongoing cultural discourse through which meanings are constituted in any given social order.

Woman is discursively constructed.
    —D.Riley, *Am I That Name? Feminism and
        the Category of "Women" in History*

Woman's place in man's life cycle has been that of nurturer, caretaker, and helpmate.
    —Carol Gilligan, *In a Different Voice:
        Psychological Theory and Women's Development*

CHAPTER 4
*Gilligan's Rhetorical
Construction of "Woman"*

As I've argued in previous chapters, whatever image of woman
we have, it grows in large measure out of discourse. In rhetorical
acts—both discursive and nondiscursive, public and private—
we encounter images of woman, which is to say we encounter
arguments for who she is, what she does, and how she is to be
regarded. Recently, a number of scholars have made a discursive
turn, increasingly infusing their work with an appreciation of
the power of language in constructing definitions of woman.
Smith (1985) offers a rationale for the focus on discourse when
she writes, "I do not think we can understand femininity as ideal
or as practice unless we understand it as a discourse . . . , unless
we understand the complexity of themes, and intertextuality,
and the character of the relation between text and she who read
it for whatever relevance it had to her everyday world" (249).
    In this chapter I pursue Smith's insight by examining in detail
a particular argument for women's nature and what their lives
should be about. It is an argument that women are and should
be oriented toward caring for others, and it was most elaborately
and persuasively put forward by Carol Gilligan in 1982. Publication of *In a Different Voice* catapulted Gilligan into the front ranks
of feminist theorizing in general and the debate over woman's
nature in particular. In it, Gilligan argues that conventional

moral theory neglects the perspective women employ in their reasoning. That viewpoint, which she labels the care perspective, prioritizes caring and responsibility to relationships, issues Gilligan reports predominate in women's thinking.

Gilligan's theory of care has inspired substantial research (Belenky, Clinchy, Goldberger, & Tarule, 1986; Eichenbaum & Orbach, 1987; Wood, 1986) and equally substantial criticism (Forum, 1986; Kittay & Meyers, 1987). Not restricted in impact to intellectual circles, *In a Different Voice* proved so popular with laypersons that it was reissued in paperback and again sold well—a notably rare feat for university press publications. Reflecting this widespread interest was *Ms.* magazine's naming of Carol Gilligan as "Woman of the Year" in 1984.

The argument Gilligan advanced reignited long-standing dissension over woman's nature. The controversy sparked by this work can be previewed by considering Gilligan's statement of purpose and some responses to it. Gilligan states early in her book that she hopes to offer women "a representation of their thought that enables them to see better its integrity and validity" (3). A number of scholars seem to agree with Gilligan that some essential qualities define women universally across time and space. Hartmann (Winkler, 1986), for instance, insists that "some factors that shape women's identity are stable and enduring" (A-6).

Many other scholars, however, argue not only that this purpose isn't achieved but that Gilligan's definition of woman is both inaccurate and regressive. Scott (1986), for instance, claims Gilligan's work is "ahistorical, defining woman/man as a universal, self-reproducing binary opposition—fixed always in the same way" (1065). Some theorists reject even the concept of woman, arguing that it is monolithic and, thus, restricts all women to only those possibilities that have been historically legitimated. Irigaray (1985) defines women by diversity: "Woman . . . is not . . . a unit(y) . . . single ideality" (229).

As these opening paragraphs indicate, a number of responses to the book and critiques of certain aspects of it have appeared. Yet, oddly, there has been no sustained critical analysis of the work's argument as it specifically contributes to current debates on woman's nature. In this chapter I offer a critical reading of *In a Different Voice.* I intend to explicate the definition of woman

Gilligan advocates and to disclose the rhetorical means by which she constructs that image. By returning to one of the key texts around which the contemporary controversy over woman's nature centers we should be able to better understand the discursive roots of the debate as well as the ongoing possibilities for using discourse to define both women and caring.

In the analysis that follows, I disclose the tension sustained between two voices, or authorial personnas, that emerge in the text: the voice of the "scholar" and the voice of the "partisan."[1] I argue that, despite her explicitly stated intent to affirm and empower women, Gilligan essentializes woman, and the particular essentialization of woman Gilligan advances invites, ironically, a restrictive and dangerously regressive view of women.

My argument proceeds first by disclosing the existence of two different and rhetorically cooperative voices in Gilligan's work. Second, I identify three rhetorical techniques Gilligan uses to construct her image of woman: First, Gilligan assumes the voice of the scholar while engaging in a variety of discursive acts that are conventionally inconsistent with that persona. Second, Gilligan relies on a rhetorical strategy of dichotomizing women and men to create simplified and oppositional portraits of the genders. Finally, Gilligan conflates historical and literary illustrations with demonstrative proofs for her claims. As she engages in each of these techniques, Gilligan relies on her ethos as a scholar to confer legitimacy on her arguments as a partisan that women are defined by their capacities to care and nurture.

Following this reading of Gilligan's work, I probe implications of the essentialized image of woman that she advances. In particular, I ask whether her advocacy of caring as a focus in women's lives is sensitive to the historical fact and ongoing potential for caring and focus on relationships to cement women's subordinate status in Western culture. If it is not, then we must ask how caring can be preserved in contemporary human communities without oppressing those who provide it.

Gilligan's Different Voices

Like the society it describes, Gilligan's book contains two voices—one dominant, the other muted. The voices are sufficiently different that each invites a distinct understanding of the text. On the one hand, the work can be read as a piece of conventional, psychological scholarship. Being authored by a faculty member at Harvard and published by its university press bestow a presumption of scholarship; and Gilligan, in one voice, reinforces this presumption by relying on vocabulary consistent with that of scholarship.

This reading is invited by the voice of the scholar who speaks with reason, qualifies inferences, supports claims made, recognizes complexities in human phenomena, and integrates understanding in a holistic manner. A clear example of this voice occurs in Gilligan's opening pages: "The different voice I describe is characterized not by gender but theme. Its association with women is an empirical observation . . . but this association is not absolute, and [does not] represent a generalization about either sex" (2). Later this voice is again apparent when Gilligan notes that "these findings were gathered at a particular moment in history, the sample was small, and the women were not selected to represent a larger population. These constraints preclude the possibility of generalization" (126). This is the voice of the scholar and, while it becomes muted in the work, it nonetheless serves to legitimize the claims of the second authorial voice.

In a Different Voice may also be read as personal advocacy for a point of view not satisfactorily supported by evidence or argument. The voice within the text that invites this reading speaks in broad generalizations, neglects and/or collapses differences to create clear categories, issues claims that exceed evidence, and relies on oppositional forms to erect dichotomous views of gender. This voice of the partisan assumes prominence in the text and, ironically, speaks in the style associated with domination and patriarchy (Penelope & Wolfe, 1983).

My analysis is predominantly grounded in Gilligan's own voice as it emerges in the 174-page book published in 1982. To a lesser extent, my analysis is informed by other scholars' commentaries on Gilligan's ideas and to specific sources with which Gilligan explicitly aligns herself. As I explore each of three rhetorical strategies upon which Gilligan relies, I simultaneously call attention to the different voices that assume ascendancy at various junctures in the text.

The Rhetorical Construction of Woman

Assuming the Voice of the "Scholar"

On first reading, *In a Different Voice* appears to be a scholarly work. This appearance is achieved not only by its association with Harvard University, but also by several passages in which Gilligan herself very carefully states the limitations of her research and warns against generalizing broadly from it. Thus, an initial presumption of scholarship is established. Yet this presumption teeters when Gilligan shifts to another voice to articulate the meaning of her research. She seems to employ the interpretive means of criticism while exceeding its purview of "theorizing the particular case" (Geertz, 1973; Leff, 1980) and, simultaneously, to seek the goal of generalizing while transgressing the methodological requirements pertinent to social science research. By thus mixing means and ends, Gilligan endangers the integrity of the voice of scholar.

Recurrent in the text are serious overgeneralizations that comprise an error in social science research and transgress the goals of criticism. This tendency is dramatically illustrated in chapter 2, devoted to describing "women's images of relationship." Citing a study she conducted with Pollak (1982), Gilligan reports that "22 percent of the women in the study added nets in the stories they wrote" about a picture of two trapeze artists (43). From this finding Gilligan concludes, "Thus, the women saw the scene on the trapeze as safe because, by providing nets, they had made it safe" (43). Since 78 percent of the women—a clear majority by any standard—did *not* add a safety net to the picture, there is no basis for claiming "the women added nets." While the conclusion Gilligan draws is unfounded, it functions to support the text's overall argument about woman's nature and inclinations. Thus, it serves the purpose of a partisan while violating basic conventions followed by scholars.

Chapter 2 also includes Gilligan's study of responses to the Heinz dilemma, a hypothetical problem used by Kohlberg (1958) in his classic study of moral development. After presenting excerpts and interpretations of two boys' and two girls' responses, Gilligan generalizes that "the structure of *boys' thought* contrasts with . . . the structure manifest in the *thought of girls*" (33, emphasis added). Gilligan's use of the strong word *manifest* implies that the structure she discerned in four cases can be generalized to represent how girls and boys in general think.

Later, Gilligan provides a single sentence in which the move from isolated examples to generalization is evident: "The two eleven-year-old children . . . presage the themes of male and female adolescent development" (49). Two children's responses, even if representative (and we have no indication that these are), do not inform about males and females in general. The problem here, as elsewhere, is not what Gilligan does per se, that is, analyze specific cases; it is rather what she suggests her methods achieve, that is, proof. Noting this in her review of Gilligan's work, Luria (1986) reasons "obviously no psychologist would object to such a technique for deriving hypotheses, but Gilligan seems, at least, to be proffering it as a basis for proof . . . the case studies through the volume cannot substitute for objectively derived data" (318). Yet it is precisely as objectively derived data that Gilligan represents her cases and as scholar that she represents herself, strategies that function rhetorically to imbue her claims with the authority of science.

Turning now to chapter 3, we find discussion of an abortion study, one of three comprising the data for the book. Initially, Gilligan assumes the scholar's voice, acknowledging that since "no effort was made to select a sample that would be representative of women considering, seeking, or having abortions," the findings cannot be interpreted as "the ways in which women in general think about the abortion choice" (72). The very page following this caveat, however, contains this broad generalization about how women in general think about abortion: "Women's constructions of the abortion dilemma in particular reveal the existence of a distinct moral language . . . [that] sets the women apart from the men whom Kohlberg studied and points toward a different understanding of moral development" (73).

This generalization recurs in the summary of chapter 3: "The abortion study demonstrates the centrality of the concepts of responsibility and care in women's constructions of the moral domain . . . and ultimately the need for an expanded developmental theory that includes . . . the feminine voice" (105). This conclusion is wholly unfounded given a sample identified as unrepresentative. Yet, from such weak evidence Gilligan argues she "demonstrates" what is central in women's moral thinking and "the need" for a major revision in established theory. In advancing it, Gilligan abandons the voice of the scholar for that of the partisan.

In addition, chapter 3 features a study of twenty-five female college students. After interpreting excerpts from only eight respondents, Gilligan issues the broad conclusion that "the essence of moral decision is the exercise of choice and the willingness to accept responsibility for that choice. To the extent that women perceive themselves as having no choice, they correspondingly excuse themselves from the responsibility that decision entails. Childlike in the vulnerability of their dependence . . ." (67). Even if we grant Gilligan's conclusion might well be informed by all twenty-five interviewees rather than the eight presented, her claims about both the essence of moral decision and the ways that women in general respond to it appear inappropriately broad. Based on only these eight responses, Gilligan later advances a stunningly broad claim: "The conflict between self and other thus constitutes the central moral problem for women" (70).

Another example of overgeneralizing from very limited data occurs in chapter 4. Again, Gilligan begins with the scholar's voice by identifying the limits of her work: "These findings were gathered at a particular moment in history, the sample was small, and the women were not selected to represent a larger population. These constraints preclude the possibility of generalization" (126). This reasonable caution about a study involving only twenty-one participants reinforces the voice of the scholar.

In the very next paragraph, however, the partisan voice emerges to offer a broad interpretation of the developmental path her study demonstrates; in so doing, she oversteps the limits she just articulated: "The changes described in women's thinking about responsibility and relationships suggest that the capacity for responsibility and care evolves through a coherent sequence of feelings and thought" (126). From here, Gilligan then generalizes beyond even the population of women considering abortion to women in general: "As the events of women's lives and history intersect with their feelings and thought, a concern with individual survival comes to be branded as selfish" (127).

In later interviews with women who contemplated abortion,

Gilligan focuses on two respondents who arrived at a "nihilistic stance." After interpreting these two accounts Gilligan states, "Moral nihilism is the conclusion . . . of women who seek, in having an abortion, to cut off their feelings" (124). Relatively short excerpts from two respondents are the sole support Gilligan offers for a major generalization about not only the women she studied but women in general who consider abortion.

A final example of the tendency to represent interpretations as proof occurs in the concluding chapter. Again, Gilligan initially qualifies her findings and, again, follows this qualification with a precarious stretch: "While the judgments considered come from a small and highly educated sample, they elucidate a contrast and make it possible to recognize not only what is missing in women's development but also what is there" (156). This statement implies her data show what is generally present in women's development, a claim unsupported by a limited, unrepresentative sample.

Throughout the text, Gilligan represents interpretations of particular cases as findings that support major generalizations. In so doing, she presents her work as "findings" of social science while simultaneously stepping outside of the methodological constraints of that genre of scholarship. She thus uses the voice of the scholar to derive legitimacy for partisan claims.

Dichotomizing Women and Men

A second rhetorical strategy upon which Gilligan relies is describing women and men in dichotomous terms. At the outset, Gilligan disavows dualistic views, telling readers that "the different voice I describe is characterized not by gender, but theme [and does not] represent a generalization about either sex" (2). This assertion, however, is quickly overshadowed both by other prefatory comments and by the juxtapositions of women and men that permeate the text.

Gilligan's dichotomous view of women and men is evident from the first page of the work, which announces that "this book records different modes of thinking about relationships and the association of these modes with male and female voices." Later, in discussing moral development, Gilligan states that "boys and girls arrive at puberty with a different interpersonal orientation and a different range of social experiences" (11).

Throughout the chapters that follow, Gilligan repeatedly high-lights differences between males and females. This strategy allows her to emphasize gender differences and overlook similarities (Tronto, 1987) so that she treats each sex as a foil for defining the other. For example, after interpreting a response from Jake, Gilligan launches her interpretation of eleven-year-old Amy's account this way: "In contrast, Amy's response to the dilemma conveys a very different impression" (27–28). Other passages offer similar evidence of a dichotomized view of the sexes: "While Jeffrey sets up a hierarchical ordering . . . , Karen describes a network of relationships. The contrasting images of hierarchy and network . . . illuminate two views of morality" (33); "To Jake's ideal of perfection . . . Amy counterposes an ideal of care. . . . While she places herself in relation to the world . . . , he places the world in relation to himself" (35); "In all of the women's descriptions, identity is defined in a context of relationship. . . . For the men, the tone of identity is different, clearer, more direct, more distinct and sharp-edged" (160). Pervading Gilligan's interpretations is language that separates men and women, contrasts them, argues they differ fundamentally in relation to one another. By relying heavily on the language of difference, Gilligan constructs a binary opposition between the women and men.

Dichotomous portraits of the sexes and their moralities are achieved not only through Gilligan's commentaries on particular accounts, but also through the larger conclusions she advances in her final chapter: that the relationship between self and other "differs in the experience of men and women . . . is a finding of my research. . . . Male and female voices typically speak the importance of different truths" (156). Underlining the contrast, Gilligan avers "the vision of maturity can be seen to shift when adulthood is portrayed by women rather than men" (167). Later, she claims, "My research suggests that men and women may speak different languages . . . [and have] disparate experiences of self and social relationships" (173). Finally, the last page of the work calls for "a greater recognition of the differences in women's experience and understanding" (174). In each of these passages Gilligan presents women as clearly distinct from men, defining each sex in opposition to the other.

Gilligan's oppositional portrayal of women and men has been recognized by other scholars. Sher (1987), for instance, contends that "Gilligan elaborates her conception of women's distinctive moral 'voice' through a series of oppositions" (179) to men's voice. Similarly, Nails (1983) suggests "a danger of the Gilligan-type . . . is that it has the power to exaggerate existing differences" (662), while Broughton (1983) laments the "dualistic psychology" inherent in Gilligan's work (635).

In addition to its tendencies to reify and oversimplify, dichotomizing is a tactic associated with androcentrism. The irony is that Gilligan develops her argument for the oppressed, subordinate group in society using "tools from the master's shed" including the voice of the dominant group. Noting this, Broughton (1983) commented that "Gilligan's separation and sharp contrast of 'male' and 'female' normative ethics and metaethics seems, in her own terms, extremely 'masculine' in its emphasis on difference and boundary, its abstraction of the mind from life, and its tendency to essentialize gender, removing it from the context of relationships, discourse, culture, societal structure, and processes of historical formation. She subscribes to the very decontextualized binary logic that elsewhere she eschews as the false consciousness of a mystifying male moiety" (635–636).

In an incisive and far-reaching analysis of the concept of gender, Scott (1986) expresses particular concern with the oppositional and, therefore, androcentric thinking of Gilligan and those who have extended her work: "It is precisely that opposition, in all its tedium and monotony, that . . . Carol Gilligan's work has promoted. . . . Gilligan's . . . notion is ahistorical, defining woman/man as a universal, self-reproducing binary opposition— fixed always in the same way. By insisting on fixed differences (in Gilligan's case, by simplifying data with more mixed results about sex and moral reasoning to underscore sexual difference), feminists contribute to the kind of thinking they want to oppose . . . binary opposition itself" (1065).

Through dichotomizing essentialized images of women and men, Gilligan establishes the base that she needs to argue the existence and value of the "different voice" of woman. Thus, the language of difference functions rhetorically to ground the text's thesis that woman has a different voice (than man).

Representing Allusions as Proof

Punctuating *In a Different Voice* are a number of literary and historical allusions. As illustrations, the allusions are interesting and could add richness and depth to more conventional scientific data; as material for critical analysis, they are appropriate if treated in ways consistent with the critical practice of understanding particular texts, not generalizing about all texts. They are not, however, the kind of empirical data required to support generalizations. Yet, it is as social science data that Gilligan (mis)represents them.

The opening chapter begins with a summary of the second act in Chekhov's *The Cherry Orchid*, followed by Gilligan's claim that the "play suggests that when the observer is a woman, the perspective may be of a different sort" (5). Later, she refers to the Persephone myth as "charting the mysterious disappearance of the female self in adolescence" (51). The problem here is not that literature cannot provide profound insight into human life, for it indisputably can. Rather, the dilemma is that Gilligan asks literary allusions to perform the work of science by presenting them as evidence of general trends in the empirical world rather than as particular, fictional accounts.

Chapter 5 offers the clearest example of (mis)representing historical and literary materials as scientific proof. Here Gilligan focuses on the relationship between women's rights and women's judgment. She anchors her analysis in two novels, George Eliot's *The Mill on the Floss* and Margaret Drabble's *The Waterfall*, without offering readers any justification for these particular selections. Of her choice to examine these two books, Gilligan says only this: "The century marked by the movement for women's rights is spanned roughly by the publication of [these] two novels, both written by women and posing the same moral dilemma" (130). With no effort to argue that these two novels represent either thinking or literature of the era, Gilligan asserts further that they "provide an historical frame in which to consider the effects of women's rights on women's moral judgment" (130).

After summarizing the two stories, Gilligan concludes that "these novels thus demonstrate the continuing power for women of the judgment of selfishness and the morality of self abnegation that it implies" (131–132). This forceful claim is issued in the voice of the scholar while being discordant with it in two ways. First, while two novels might well illustrate or suggest something, they do not—cannot—"demonstrate" a broad empirical reality as Gilligan explicitly claims they do. Further, after seeing the conclusion Gilligan draws from these novels, a reader might reasonably question their representativeness, asking why she did not select works by Virginia Woolf, Charlotte Perkins Gilman, Marge Piercy, Flannery O'Connor, or Alice Walker, whose characters seem less plagued by fears of being judged selfish.

Gilligan then introduces Wollstonecraft and Stanton as feminist activists concerned with the power of judgments in women's rights. Most informed readers will grant the appropriateness of Gilligan's selection of these women as activists in the first wave of feminism, although a reasonable question could be raised about whether they represent women of their time. Even if this question is not raised, two novels and two activists from a hundred-year span offer a tenuous basis for the generalization that "the moral conflicts described by contemporary women . . . demonstrate the continuation through time of an ethic of responsibility as the center of women's moral concern" (132). On the basis of four women, Gilligan claims to "demonstrate" (prove) what is "the" (not a) moral concern of women (not two extraordinary women and two fictional characters in a single century).

In closing the chapter on women's rights, Gilligan claims that "a comparison of dilemmas described by three of the women shows, across a wide range of formulations, how the opposition between selfishness and responsibility complicates for women the issue of choice" (138). Finally, she ends the chapter by informing readers that "thus changes in women's rights change women's moral judgments" (149). By representing isolated literary and historical characters as support for empirical generalizations, Gilligan suggests a scholarly basis for her claims that in fact, does not exist in her text.

Realizing the "potential influence of this [Gilligan's] work in characterizing women's thinking," Luria (1986) finds it "imperative to scrutinize the bases of its arguments and to ask whether the evidence is yet sufficient to warrant Gilligan's conclusions" (316). Doing so leads Luria to the judgment that "the weaving of literary examples (presumably as metaphors), theoretical proposal, and loosely defined empirical research can be a winning

but seductive design; occasionally Gilligan does not draw a clear
line between theoretical speculation and discussion of data slips
from hunch, example, or metaphor to 'proven fact'" (316). Scott
(1986) reaches a similar conclusion, arguing that Gilligan's work
evidences a "slippage that often happens in the attribution of
causality: the argument moves from a statement such as 'women's
experience leads them to make moral choices contingent on contexts and relationships' to 'women think and choose this way
because they are women'" (1065). As partisan, Gilligan may
believe that women are essentially oriented toward caring; as a
scholar, she does not prove the claim.

I am suggesting that the two voices are rhetorically cooperative
in that the initial voice of the scholar confers legitimacy on the
voice of the partisan who dominates the text as a whole. To
establish this credibility, Gilligan assumes the role of the scholar
early in the book to note quite explicitly that her data do not allow
generalization. Yet, as partisan she does generalize, sometimes
sweepingly, in violation of her own scholarly caveat. This judgment is shared by others who have studied Gilligan's work. After
reviewing original transcripts comprising the data for *In a Different Voice*, Nails (1983) reported that Gilligan tended to collapse
respondents' thoughts in ways more consistent with the view of
women she endorses than the respondents' accounts. This and
other methodological problems in Gilligan's book led Nails to the
harsh conclusion that *In a Different Voice* is based on "underlying
assumptions so shaky that no amount of intellectual scaffolding
could support them" (655). Similarly, Luria's assessment of Gilligan's work is that rather than being the empirically supported
theory its author represents it as, the book is "a somewhat impres-
sionistic grouping of the stories Gilligan's subjects told" (318).
What Nails and Luria did not point out is what the above reading
reveals: the voice of the scholar creates legitimacy for that of the
partisan by wrapping loose claims of advocacy within the guise
of scholarly language.

Gilligan's Construction of Woman as Caring and "Response-able"

Gilligan clearly intended her work to enhance appreciation of
women and caring, a goal explicated in the introduction: "For

women, I hope this work will offer a representation of their thought that enables them to see better its integrity and validity" (3). In her concluding chapter, Gilligan reaffirms this purpose: "I want to restore in part the missing text of women's development" (156). Yet, the nature of the "missing text" Gilligan wants to restore is an essentialist view of woman that has dangerously regressive implications.

Gilligan identifies the missing text as a "conception of morality as concerned with the activity of care [that] centers moral development around the understanding of responsibility and relationships" (19). Explicitly linking this morality to women, Gilligan claims it emerges "when one begins with the study of women and derives developmental constructs from their lives" (19). She further asserts that "woman's place in man's life cycle is to protect this recognition . . . of the continuing importance of attachment" (23). In her concluding chapter, Gilligan reinforces the association between women and caring, writing that women "define their identity through relationships of intimacy and care" (164); and "women's development delineates . . . a maturity realized through interdependence and taking care" (172). By presenting the care ethic as derived from and definitive of women, Gilligan essentializes women in general as caring and responsible to others. A reading of the text clarifies Gilligan's meanings for the two terms central to her construction of woman: caring and responsiveness, or responsibility.

Caring as Constitutive of Woman

Early in the text Gilligan indicates her comfort with roles historically assigned to women: "Women's place in man's life cycle has been that of nurturer, caretaker, and helpmate" (17). She then identifies "care for and sensitivity to the needs of others" as "traits that have traditionally defined the 'goodness' of women" (18). Embracing the cultural legacy of women, Gilligan further defines caring by noting that "from a care perspective, detachment is *the* moral problem" (31). Other passages illuminating what Gilligan means by care as a quality of woman state that "women define their identity through relationships of intimacy and care" (164); "the ideal of care is thus an activity of relationship, of seeing and responding to need, taking care of the world" (62); "the expression of care is seen as the fulfillment of moral responsibility" (73); and "the conventional feminine voice emerges with great clarity, defining the self and proclaiming its worth on the basis of the ability to care for and protect others. . . . The strength of this position lies in its capacity for caring" (79). In these statements Gilligan defines care as constitutive of woman, her morality, and her worth.

Responsibility as Constitutive of Woman

Responsibility is the other term concerning the image of women that Gilligan's advances. Initially, Gilligan equates this with the "obligation to exercise care and avoid hurt" (73). Later, she elaborates the "morality of responsibility" as one "that knits such claims [of individuals] into a fabric of relationship, blurring the distinction between self and other through the representation of their interdependence" (132). In the closing chapter, Gilligan further clarifies: "The ethic of responsibility rests on an understanding that gives rise to compassion and care" (165). These passages suggest that responsibility involves experiencing others' needs as one's own, which, as we saw in the preceding chapter, is one of the requirements of caring and has the potential to diminish a caregiver's autonomy and sensitivity to her or his own motives, needs, and goals.

Inherent in Gilligan's definition of woman as responsible and caring is acceptance of a traditional view of women as reactive rather than proactive. While at one point Gilligan attempts to dissociate her view of caring from responsiveness, other parts of the text as well as its overall weight support an interpretation of her image of woman as responsive. Initially, Gilligan says caring should be adopted out of free choice: "When the distinction between helping and pleasing frees the activity of taking care from the wish for approval by others, the ethic of responsibility can become a self-chosen anchor of personal integrity and strength" (171). In this passage Gilligan directly links the integrity of caring to its being freely chosen. Yet one page later Gilligan undermines the possibility of women's making a free choice to care in a culture that has socialized them to regard others and relationships as primary in their lives: "The reality of connection is experienced by women as *a given rather than as freely contracted*" (172; emphasis added).

Gilligan's endorsement of a view of women as responsive is further supported by evidence extrinsic to the text but directly reflective of her position. In a 1987 clarification of the book, Gilligan states that "care is grounded in the assumption that self and other are interdependent, an assumption reflected in a view of action as responsive and, therefore, as arising in relationships rather than the view of action as emanating from within the self and, therefore, 'self governed.' Seen as responsive, the self is by definition connected to others" (24; also Gilligan, 1986). In this later statement, Gilligan contradicts her original claim that to have integrity care must be freely chosen, and she endorses a responsive identity for caregivers.

To fully understand Gilligan's position on the responsiveness of caring, it is instructive to recover one of the primary sources upon which she draws. Gilligan relies explicitly and heavily on the work of Jean Baker Miller for the theoretical foundation of her construction of woman. Gilligan quotes a passage from Miller to anchor her own initial discussion of women's morality: "Women stay with, build on, and develop in a context of attachment and affiliation with others, . . . women's sense of self becomes very much organized around being able to make, and then to maintain, affiliations and relationships. . . . This psychic starting point contains the possibilities for an entirely different (and more advanced) approach to living and functioning . . . affiliation is valued as highly as, or more highly than, self-enhancement" (Miller, 1976, 83; quoted in Gilligan, 1982, 169–170). In the sentence immediately following this quote, Gilligan represents Miller's position as supportive of her own: "Thus, Miller points to a psychology of adulthood which recognizes that development does not displace the value of ongoing attachment and the continuing importance of care in relationships" (169–170).

When we return to the source, however, we find Miller's meaning is not fully and fairly rendered by Gilligan's. Clearly Miller does value women as well as affiliations and caring; yet Miller's position is more qualified, more reserved, and more balanced than Gilligan's representation of it implies. Three pages after the passage Gilligan quoted, Miller (1986) suggests the centrality of affiliation in women's lives is, at best, a mixed blessing: "Women do face a problem, one that troubles them greatly, the problem arises from the dominant role affiliations have been made to play in women's lives" (86). Especially revealing in this comment is Miller's choice of the passive voice ("have been made to play"), which suggests the role of affiliations in women's lives is imposed, not self-chosen. Continuing further in the chapter from which Gilligan quoted, Miller offers this tempered view: "Women's great desire for affiliation is both a fundamental strength . . . and at the same time the inevitable source of many of women's current problems. . . . When women act on the basis of this underlying psychological motive [for affiliation], they are usually led into subservience" (89). Here also Miller's language reveals that she believes women have a lack of choice in the roles they are "led into."

Further reading of Miller's book illuminates the fact that she is not unambiguously supportive of women's roles in caring. Fairly early in her discussion of women's psychology, for example, Miller (1986) clearly states she does not encourage traditional roles for women: "I do not imply that women should go back to some supportive role. *It is the reverse*" (47; emphasis added). Other passages reinforce this stance: "Women have been so encouraged to concentrate on the emotions and reactions of others that they have been diverted from examining and expressing their own emotions" (39); "Women . . . have come to believe that they should *want* to respond at all times and in all ways" (51); "The characteristics most highly developed in women and perhaps most essential to human beings are *the* very characteristics that are specifically dysfunctional for success in the world as it is" (124). Miller's valuing of women's tradition as caregivers is seasoned by awareness of how those qualities and those who enact them fare in society.

Finally, Miller's position is distinct from Gilligan's in dynamism. Gilligan seems to view traditional womanly qualities as static, qualities women have always had and that have always been undervalued but whose unchanging merit nonetheless ennobles them. This is not what Miller assumes. While she does agree with Gilligan that caring and affiliation have traditionally dominated women's lives and that both have been devalued in our culture, she stops short of using women to celebrate or cultivate them.

Rather, she argues, "These characteristics can be seen as valuable *only* as they are also seen in a dynamic state, moving toward something more" (123).

This comparison of Miller's and Gilligan's texts discloses some incompatibilities between the two. Unlike Gilligan, Miller situates traditionally womanly qualities within the context of culture, leading her to recognize that, intrinsic merit not withstanding, they have been and continue to be liabilities for women in "the world as constituted" (Miller, 125). Miller also does not view women as necessarily or desirably characterized primarily by caring and attachment to others while Gilligan does. Thus, Miller's regard for women's traditional roles and qualities is both contextualized and qualified; Gilligan's is neither.

In celebrating women's role as caregiver as what has always been "woman's place in man's life cycle," Gilligan grants women only a place—and one of service at that—in a life designed by men. Thus, Gilligan not only removes women's traditional roles from historical and cultural contexts, but also totalizes limited aspects of some women to construct a simplified image of all women. By representing advocacy as scholarship, dichotomizing men and women, and conflating literary and historical allusions with proof, Gilligan constructs an image of woman that holds open no space for diversity, exceptions, or change.

The woman Gilligan constructs is a caregiver, defined by and responsible to relationships.[2] Gilligan's essentialization of these features of woman is especially evident in her final chapter where the voice of the partisan dominates: "Women depict ongoing attachment as the path that leads to maturity . . . to see themselves as women is to see themselves in a relationship of connection" (171); "Women's development delineates the path not only to a less violent life but also to a maturity realized through interdependence and taking care" (172). It is revealing that Gilligan consistently uses the definite article to imply attachment is of singular importance in women's lives; it is *the* single path (not one of many) that characterizes women's (not some women's) development.

In the closing pages of *In a Different Voice*, the two authorial voices cooperate to represent the partisan's essentialist view as that of a scholar: "Given the evidence of different perspectives in the representations of adulthood by women and men . . . in the different voice of women lies the truth of an ethic of care, the tie between relationship and responsibility" (173). In claiming that *the* voice of women offers *the* truth of caring as *the* tie between relationship and responsibility, Gilligan promotes monolithic views of both sexes and, further, represent these as "given" by "the evidence." Broad claims that exceed data would not be issued in the voice of a scholar.

Thus, despite Gilligan's opening statement that her work does not "represent a generalization about either sex" (2), throughout the text she advances generalizations. *In a Different Voice* constructs an essentialist view of woman. The image of women that Gilligan promotes is a problem not only because of its shaky empirical base, but also because of its relation to larger questions about women and their roles in society.

Gilligan's Place Within the Essentialist Debate

The significance of Gilligan's text is more fully disclosed when it is placed within two horizons. First, her construction of a generalized woman should be understood within the major current discourse on essentializing woman. Second, the particular essentialization of woman that Gilligan advances must be considered within historical and cultural horizons of meaning.

In their influential history of feminist thought, Eisenstein and Jardine (1980) note that in the 1970s an essentialist view of woman emerged as a reaction to liberal feminists' deemphasis of differences between women and men as a strategy for increasing women's participation in professional and sociopolitical life. Challenging this view, the essentialists sought to reclaim and valorize qualities and activities traditionally associated with woman.

Essentialist views of woman reflect at least three influences. First, they bespeak interest in imbuing with value a distinctively feminine-based space and identity within an androcentric society. Of this position, Young (1985) notes it "argues for the superiority of values embodied in traditionally female experience, and rejects the values embodied in traditionally male dominated institutions" (173). Essentialist views also heighten unity among women

both for purposes of sisterhood/support and political organizing
and action. Winkler (1988) observes that a focus on "differences
among women, for example, makes it difficult to forge a unified
feminist politics" (A-7).[3] Finally, the inclination toward a universal conception of woman partakes of the quest for unity inherent
in conventional science and is endorsed by those who "are uncomfortable with a theory that denies the possibility of unity" (Winkler, 1988, A-6).

Initial enthusiasm for a unified view of woman, however,
waned as scholars increasingly recognized its dangers. Bluntly
stating reservations to an essentialist concept, deLaurelis (1984)
distinguishs between "woman . . . a fictional construct, a distillate
from diverse but congruent discourses dominant in Western
culture" and "women . . . the real historical beings" (5). Kristeva
(1982) goes further to call for the culture "to break free of its
belief in Woman, Her power, Her writing, so as to channel this
demand for difference into each and every element of the female
whole, and, finally, to bring out the singularity of each woman
and, beyond this, her multiplicities" (51; also see Kristeva, 1974,
1981).[4] Kristeva's statement illustrates the increasing concern
that essentialist views of woman constrict what society and women
themselves perceive as options for women. Commenting on this,
Ferguson (1988) notes that some theorists see "in the totalizing
impulse a duplication of the practices of power and fearing that
such practices will force us to hide from ourselves that which
does not fit into our schemas" (76–77).

Perhaps the most serious challenge to essentialist views comes
from women of color who claim that female nature is both not
universal and not appropriately considered in isolation from
other key aspects of identity, notably race and class. Henderson
(Winkler, 1988) observes that "an exclusively gendered analysis
is the privilege of a homogeneous society in which the individual
and society are one. In a heterogeneous society it is highly problematical, particularly for those people on the margins" (A-5).
This failure of inclusion has led others to charge essentialist views
of women are both biased and elitist. In a sharp indictment of
existing theory, Stanback (1988) argues "'Liberal' or 'bourgeois
feminism'. . . is inappropriate to the study of black women because it is neither systemic nor inclusive. . . . Liberal feminism
represents white middle-class women's success in universalizing

their experience of womanhood. . . . It excludes important aspects of the black female experience" (29). Not only suspect in terms of bias and elitism, then, Gilligan's theory, based on a very limited and nonrepresentative sample of white women, is open to questions of basic validity. The exclusion of nonwhite women from her sample is particular ironic since Gilligan based her work on the complaint that conventional moral theory was flawed by its exclusion of women.

Feminist theorists' concern with essentialist views of woman provides a horizon for evaluating *In a Different Voice*. To the extent that Gilligan offers a generalized description of woman that totalizes care and "response-ability," her work contributes to an essentializing, and, therefore, restrictive view of women. Criticizing this, Nails (1983) argues "The Gilligan-type description of female moral development . . . can erect a set of boundaries for female moral development, a set of limits on behavior: a girl child who sees a moral dilemma as 'sort of like a math problem with humans' (a response of one of Gilligan's male sixth graders) is viewed as somehow less feminine than one who emphasizes the relationships among the various characters" (663). To the extent that women themselves accept Gilligan's image of them, they risk limiting their options, actions, and identities.

A second horizon that enhances understanding and evaluation of Gilligan's argument is its sociohistorical context. As with any activity, caring and the responsibility ethic underlying it are defined not by absolute criteria, but by cultural values, historical meanings, and social role assignments. Within the context of Western society, giving care is a historically devalued activity, one relegated to subordinates. Those not in positions of power are expected (sometimes required) to understand, minister to, and be concerned about others. Recognizing this, Miller (1986) bluntly states that "in our culture 'serving others' is for losers, it is low-level stuff" (61). Thus, to encourage women to define themselves by their capacities to care and respond to others is to reinforce their traditionally subordinate, tentative positions in society; it also undercuts critical reflection on these roles (Sommers & Shields, 1987).

Gilligan recognizes the dangers that caring can pose for women when she concedes that "the notion that virtue for women lies in self sacrifice has complicated women's development" (132). She nevertheless argues caring should be valued and enacted because of its intrinsic merit, regardless of social interpretations and consequences. She maintains, for instance, "that women's embeddedness in lives of relationship, their orientation to interdependence, their subordination of achievement to care, and their conflicts over competitive success leave them more personally at risk in mid-life seems more a commentary on the society than a problem in women's development" (171). Gilligan's dismissal of historical and cultural contexts seems facile and, in Dubois's (1980) judgment, fails to "address the limitation of the values of women's culture including the ways in which they constrain women" (31). Historically, Western society has not bestowed value on the roles traditionally assigned to women through any of the rewards and privileges that sustain social hierarchies. So long as what is associated with and encouraged in women is not accorded widespread respect and so long as it serves the comfort and convenience of those who enjoy positions of power, then the roles and activities will continue to allow oppression and exploitation (Campbell 1973, 1983; Welter, 1966). In an incisive analysis of affirmations of woman's traditional sphere, Alcoff (1988) concludes,

> To the extent that cultural feminism merely valorizes genuinely positive attributes developed under oppression, it cannot map our long-range course. To the extent that it reinforces essentialist explanations of these true attributes, it is in danger of solidifying an important bulwark of sexist oppression: the belief in an innate "womanhood" to which we must all adhere lest we be deemed either inferior or not "true women." (414)

In a Different Voice cannot be understood apart from this social history of Western society. Once placed within this horizon of meaning, Gilligan's essentialized view of woman can be understood as reiterating and revalorizing the definition of woman that has been resoundingly oppressive historically. The work, then, contributes to maintenance of oppression rather than challenging or reforming the symbolic and social structures and practices that sustain it.[5] The qualities and roles traditionally assigned to women can be enacted without harm to women only if strategies for gaining broad cultural legitimation and value are developed and successfully deployed. This underscores the wisdom of Miller's equivocal view of traditional womanly qualities as dynamic and valuable only as they lead to further development of women and the society in which they participate.

In this chapter I have argued that while Gilligan represents her book as scholarship, it is better understood as a work of advocacy. Within the text there is sustained tension between two rhetorically cooperative voices in which the author speaks. Disclosing the presence of these two voices and the ways in which they interact to create the overall meaning of the text challenges both the text's scholarly nature and its value to women.

It is in the voice of the scholar that Gilligan introduces *In a Different Voice* as a "report of research in progress" (3). Yet a second voice, that of the partisan, becomes audible early and assumes increasing prominence as the text unfolds. As partisan, Gilligan advances an essentialist view of woman as defined by caring and "response-ability," qualities that Gilligan encourages in women despite their historical devaluation. What makes this argument persuasive is its appearance as scholarship, rather than advocacy. Gilligan uses the voice of the scholar to establish the legitimacy of the claims of the partisan. By disclosing the strategies Gilligan employs to construct an essentialized image of woman, I have tried to provide insight into how the book works and, at the same time, to suggest scholarly and pragmatic limitations in Gilligan's argument for woman's invariant nature as a caregiver.

This is not to say what Gilligan describes as womanly qualities are not intrinsically valuable and, perhaps, essential to human survival. Yet, it is the case that these qualities can be inculcated and enacted without harm to the actors if and only if strategies for gaining broad cultural legitimation and valuing of caring accompany affirmations like Gilligan's.

In this chapter I have focused on one work out of the many on caring, because Gilligan's book is particularly significant to my overall inquiry. It is so because, more than any other single publication, *In A Different Voice* reinvigorated traditional conceptions of women as caregivers. Thus, Gilligan and her work may be regarded as representing one important position in the contemporary debate over women's roles and women's ways. Both what Gilligan argues—that women have been and should be the primary caregivers and relationship builders in our society—and how she argues this position—through essentializing women and viewing them out of historical, political, social, and economic contexts of meaning—must be understood in order to inquire further into the relationships among women, care, and culture.

In the next chapter I consider further Gilligan's largely implied view of the source of women's caregiving inclinations. In addition, I explore other views of the genesis of tendencies to care. Through examining different arguments for the basis of caring we may gain insight into the necessity, or nonnecessity, of the entrenched association between women and caregiving.

Women's deference is rooted in . . . the substance of her moral concerns: sensitivity to the needs of others and the assumption of responsibility for taking care.

—Carol Gilligan, *In a Different Voice: Psychological Theory and Women's Development*

It comes down, in the end, to . . . recognition of other people's needs. The subordinate learns it because they have to.

—Elizabeth Janeway, *Man's World, Woman's Place: A Study in Social Mythology*

Because women are themselves mothered by women, they grow up with the relational capacities and needs, and psychological definition of self-in-relationship, which commits them to mothering.

—Nancy Chodorow, *The Reproduction of Mothering: Psychoanalysis and the Sociology of Gender*

Through gender relations two types of persons are created: man and woman.

—Jane Flax, "Postmodernism and Gender Relations in Feminist Theory"

CHAPTER 5
The Genesis of Women's Tendency to Care

How do we explain who the caregivers are? Our everyday experiences and observations reveal to us that not everyone seems inclined to care for others to the same degree. We notice that some people seem more prone to be caring individuals than others. Do we account for this by an appeal to natural or genetic factors, assuming that the tendency to care, like the color of eyes and body height, is somehow prewired in some people? Alternatively, do we invoke various social-psychological explanations, saying some individuals are taught to care while others are not or some people have role models of caring that are not accessible to others? Neither of these explanations sheds much light on the relatively systematic patterns we see in who cares in the United States. How do we explain our everyday observation that those who care are disproportionately women and are subordinate in social status?

The quotations at the start of this chapter represent a sample of answers that have been given to the question of who cares. Prior chapters have also suggested some of the different answers that have been advanced to explain who cares and why they care. Gilligan, like the mourners at my mother's funeral, accepts women's pronounced tendency to care for others as rooted in their basic personality development and integral to what women have always been. But is the tendency to care adequately explained by appeals to sex or even to the constructed nature of gender? Do we accept Gilligan's view of women as caregivers and her implied argument that women simply value others more than men do?

Gilligan's constructions of women and caring are not uncontroversial. Alternate explanations of women's demonstrated tendency to care for others have been proffered and merit our attention if we are to understand what caring means and who does it. In this chapter I examine major explanations of who cares to see how any or all of them might enlarge our understanding of caring by illuminating the circumstances that give rise to it.

My goal is to historicize caring in order to allow us to appreciate the ways it has been situated in and promoted by psychological, social, political, historical, and economic conditions. By doing this I plan to gain some insight into the circumstances that foster a tendency to care for others and, with that, the development of concrete skills such as empathy, nurturance, and an ability to let go of egocentric preoccupations. A satisfying account of caring should also illuminate marked patterns by revealing why it is that women and people with subordinate status have, at least historically, been most expected as well as most likely to care for others.

To launch this effort we concentrate on the three most prominent explanations that have been advanced for the tendency to care.[1] First, we return to Gilligan's claim that an ethic of caring[2] is rooted in family dynamics, which, because they are distinct for male and female infants, foster differential tendencies for caring in the two sexes. A second explanation lodges the tendency to care in pervasive socialization processes that teach gender and, with that, the expectation that caring for others is part of the female, but not the male role. Finally, our attention focuses on an explanation firmly rooted in the social structure itself, specifically prevailing power relationships of which gender is an important category.

We then consider the limits of each and all of these explanations in informing us about the origins of caring as it is understood and practiced in diverse ways and situations. In turn, understanding these limits should allow us to address larger questions about the very way that we conceive questions about the relationship between women and caring in the United States. How credible we find any explanation of the tendency to care has important implications for what care really means and, perhaps, for how its enmeshed association with women in Western culture can be contested if we so choose.

Care as a Function of Family Dynamics: "The Reproduction of Mothering"

Nancy Chodorow's influential book, *The Reproduction of Mothering: Psychoanalysis and the Sociology of Gender* (1978) argues, as the title suggests, that the relationship between infants and their primary caregivers, usually mothers, creates an identification between mothers and daughters within which mothers reproduce in daughters the tendencies to nurture and care for others. This view, which I discussed briefly in chapter 3, claims that because a daughter defines herself in relation to another, she develops a relational sense of self and an attentiveness to others and their needs.

In important ways, insist Chodorow and others studying childhood development, the mother-daughter bond is different from that between mother and son. In daughters, writes Chodorow, mothers see themselves and want to reproduce themselves; in sons mothers see someone different from who they are and, thus, do not attempt to reproduce themselves in the males. In mother-child interactions the mother accentuates and promotes identification[3] with a daughter while the mother and son recognize and act on their difference from one another, an early development that is then elaborated in family dynamics to fashion distinctive identities for male and female children. Thus, concludes Chodorow in the final passage of her analysis, "Because women are themselves mothered by women, they grow up with the relational capacities and needs . . . which commits [sic] them to mothering. Men, because they are mothered by women, do not" (209).

In an early formulation of this hypothesis, Chodorow (1974) theorizes that "the fact that women, universally, are largely responsible for early child care" accounts for "the reproduction within each generation of certain general and nearly universal differences that characterize masculine and feminine personality and roles" (43–44). Thus, mothering reproduces mothering, which is understood as a general inclination to care for others.

Continuing this theme in her later and best-known work, Chodorow (1978) argues that the early interaction and the identification between mother and daughter is pivotal in making caring for others a priority in women's lives. "Because mothers are the same gender as their daughters and have been girls," writes Chodorow, "mothers of daughters tend not to experience these infant daughters as separate from them in the same way as do mothers of infant sons. . . . Mothers normally identify more with daughters and experience them as less separate" (109). The daughter's experiences—this intense relationship with her mother—lead her to identify with, to feel one with, her mother.

In one of her most recent statements, Chodorow (1990) repeats her argument that "as a result of being parented primarily by a woman, men and women develop differently constructed selves and different experiences of their gender and gender identity. Through their early relationship with their mother, women develop a sense of self continuous with others. . . . This psychic structure and self-other process in turn help to reproduce mothering" (119).

Because males are mothered differently, they develop different senses of self and, with those, a generally less caring orientation toward others. An observable difference is that males are not held as close physically or psychologically as are female infants. Further, and particularly important from the psychoanalytic standpoint, males recognize that they are not like their mothers. They cannot identify themselves with their mothers: they cannot use a female model to define their identities. Thus, to develop a sense of themselves, boys must differentiate from their mothers; they define themselves by separating from this first relationship. Summarizing how these differential developmental processes affect later tendencies to be involved with others, Chodorow (1978) writes, "Relational abilities and preoccupations have been extended in women's development and curtailed in men's" (169). The developmental dynamics for males, then, encourage separation from others and a view of self as independent, neither of which provides much basis for interpersonal sensitivities, such as empathy, which seem essential to feelings of compassion and caring for others.

Chodorow's work acknowledges its substantial debt to Stoller's (1964) research, which concludes that gender identity is an extremely firm core of personality that is almost invariably established by the age of three (1964). If Stoller is correct in the primacy and centrality of gender identity, then it would presumably be heavily influenced by mother-child interactions. Because the mother-child relationship is both the first and putatively one of the most important, its influence is extraordinary. Thus, the understandings of self and how to relate to others formed in this bond establish a central foundation that guides most, if not all, future relationships.

According to psychoanalytic theory, this accounts for the adult proclivities of males to maintain distance from others and to be generally less aware of and sensitive to others' feelings and for females to create relationships of closeness that entail substantial understanding of others. In this way, family psychodynamic processes explain male and female development and, relatedly, the marked tendency of females to feel more connected to others and to be more inclined to care for them.

This account also offers an explanation of broadly shared expectations that women should care for others. Because mothers are constantly attentive and responsive to infants' needs, Chodorow (1978) asserts, both "girls and boys expect and assume women's unique capacities for sacrifice, caring, and mothering" (83). Early interactions with mothers form "conscious and unconscious attitudes and expectations that all people—male and female—have of their mothers in particular, and of women in general" (91). Infant personality development, then, affects not only how one defines self but how one defines others and relationships with them.

Miller, another clinician, also emphasizes family dynamics in her account of key differences in feminine and masculine personalities, including the more relational self-characteristic of females. In the foreword to the second edition of her influential *A New Psychology of Women*, Miller (1986) reiterates her interest in the "'relational contexts' and 'relational modes' which foster psychological development" for female infants (xxiii). Later Miller returns to this issue to note that from what is known about "development of a person's fundamental sense of identity, it is linked very early with her/his sense of being a female or male person. . . . We come to link our sense of existence with a sexed existence so early that we cannot even think of ourselves as simply a 'person.' We can only think, 'I am a so and so, a man,' or 'so and so, a woman'" (71). The gendered identity that females develop, Miller continues, "is rooted in the encouragement to 'form' themselves into the person who will be of benefit to others. . . . This experience begins at birth." (73). Miller, like Chodorow, points to the earliest stages of life as the context that gives rise to females' tendency to care for, or mother, others.

Common to each of these writers is the focus on family psychodynamics as primary in shaping identity and, with that, the pronounced tendency to care for others more empirically characteristic of women. Clearly, it makes intuitive sense to assume that the highly formative relationship between mother and child influences the child's sense of self, including gender identity and associated qualities such as empathy in females and independence in males. And, in fact, few have voiced disagreement with the claim that the mother-child relationship is fundamentally influential.

The major challenge to this viewpoint questions not its explanation of what happens in infancy, nor even its arguments about the extensive, life-long implications of the mother-child relationship for personality and adult behavior patterns. Instead, what is contested is whether this explanation is adequate in scope to explain why the mother herself is oriented toward care. Chodorow would respond by pointing out that the mother herself was mothered and this explains why she is caring, but of course this misses the point of the criticism. At some point capacities involved in caring—nurturing, responsiveness, defining self in relationship to others—came to be regarded as distinctive of femininity. The failure to explain how this came about is the problem for those who regard the psychodynamic explanation as limited in explanatory power.

Rather than being the basic cause of tendencies to care, some critics suggest, what transpires in mother-child relationships might be better conceived a mediating influence. Put another way, the issue is whether family actually creates gender identity or only recreates it by passing on the values and definitions of the culture at large. From the latter perspective, the family is understood as an agency of society entrusted to socialize children by inculcating in them the roles, meanings, and so forth formulated in and constitutive of the broader context.

This understanding that families are embedded in a larger culture is clearly assumed in both Miller and Chodorow's work, although this has not always been recognized. While their analyses focus on psychodynamics within families, both clinicians recognize that the family is situated within a larger culture that establishes what counts as femininity and masculinity. Chodorow (1978), for example, states, "I argue that the contemporary reproduction of mothering occurs through social structurally induced psychological processes" (6), a focus that clearly acknowledges the influence of social organization on family patterns. Throughout *The Reproduction of Mothering*, Chodorow makes reference to the existing organization of society and the gendered roles upon which it insists. Similarly, Miller views both women's tendencies to care and devaluation of that activity as reflective of Western culture's structure and ideology, which separate private relationships from public life and assign women and men accordingly to these two spheres.

A fair reading of Chodorow and Miller reveals that they acknowledge the surrounding culture as a critical source of meanings, which are internalized in and passed on within families. It is telling, in this regard, that Chodorow herself designates her account as an explanation of the reproduction of mothering, not the production of mothering. In describing her analysis this way, Chodorow hints that broad cultural processes and practices are substantially implicated in the meanings of motherhood and, more generally, feminine orientations.

Gilligan (1982), however, discusses family psychodynamics as the essential cause of tendencies to care for others, a view less qualified than that of Miller or Chodorow. Her explanation of women's care ethic focuses centrally and virtually exclusively on family dynamics that are different for male and female infants. The section of her book dealing with reinterpretations of Freudian theory (primarily as put forward by Chodorow and Miller), in fact, comprises her only effort at establishing a theoretical foundation for her claims of women's difference (chap. 1). Unlike Chodorow and Miller, however, Gilligan lifts the psychodynamic processes she discusses out of the context of the larger society within which families are situated. This implies that processes of identification and introjection themselves are basic "causes" of tendencies to care. Gilligan further decontextualizes her analysis by rigidly juxtapositioning the tendency to care against the justice-oriented values that she suggests are more characteristic of males and society as a whole. In so doing, she isolates females' development from the culture at large and, thus, upholds the age-old dichotomy between public and private spheres of life and associated male and female ways of being.

Important to our inquiry is realizing that in drawing on Miller and Chodorow's explanations of how family dynamics operate, Gilligan misinterprets their perspective and, consequently, she misrepresents the essence of their claims. Both clinicians quite explicitly assume cultural forces shape and are manifest within families,[4] but they chose to focus their analysis on what happens in families, that is, how social values are communicated and reproduced in children through particular family dynamics.

Gilligan, however, limits her inferences from Miller and Chodorow's work to their elucidations of psychodynamic patterns in mother-child relationships. With that selective foundation, Gilligan's own work treats caring and gender as qualities of individuals developed in specific families; her explanation never exceeds individual psychology and family dynamics, never locates these phenomena within larger social systems and, thus, fails to recognize that both gender and caring are thoroughly social constructs—ideas that are created by and through the interactions among members of a culture.

In response to Gilligan's grounding of explanation in family psychodynamics, Joan Scott (1986) criticizes the position's "literalism, its reliance on relatively small structures of interaction to produce gender identity and to generate change. . . . This interpretation limits the concept of gender to family and household experience and . . . leaves no way to connect the concept (or the individual) to other social systems of economy, politics, or power" (1062–1063). Scott hammers home her criticisms by arguing that we cannot understand much of what gender is in any culture unless we give serious "attention to symbolic systems, that is, to the ways societies represent gender, use it to articulate the rules of social relationships, or construct the meaning of experience" (1063).

In essence, what Scott and others critical of the emphasis on family psychodynamics want to do is to situate socialization and psychological practices that occur inside families within the larger and, they believe, more analytically important context of society. In calling for this enlargement of the scene, they hope to point the way to a more comprehensive understanding of the development of gender and, particularly, care orientations as not merely individual phenomena nor manifestations of specific family dynamics, but rather systematic reproductions of cultural patterns that differentiate genders and prescribe roles to be adopted by females and males.

Caring as Rooted in Feminine Socialization

If we grant that gender is social, not merely individual, then social life suggests itself as the genesis of a gendered self-concept and, specifically, caring as a feminine tendency. This is precisely the point of view taken by a number of individuals who find family psychodynamics incomplete as an explanation of why women tend to care for others more than men.

Early work in this area focused on sex and/or gender in studies, treating it as a quality of individuals. This led to a spate of findings about differences between men and women in particular contexts and on particular measures. Yet this approach was unable either to illuminate how observed differences arise or to demonstrate how those differences are related systematically to social systems within which individuals are located. Criticisms of this perspective focused on the inaccuracy of treating sex or gender as a quality that varies within individuals. Elsewhere I have argued that to treat sex or gender as simply a variable "represents it as only an individual quality, like green eyes or I.Q. This definition of sex ignores the larger fact that gender . . . is a property of social structures, beliefs and practices" (1993).

More recent thinking about the ways gender is socialized reflects understanding of gender as an analytic category that "permeates and defines all aspects of human interaction . . . because of the ways in which it is defined, valued, and generally contextualized within a given society" (Wood, 1993). Relatively new in intellectual history, the idea of gender as an analytic category appeared only in the second half of the present century. From this viewpoint, gender is understood "as a way of talking about systems of social or sexual identity" (Scott, 1986). In its most broad sense, this perspective is concerned with understanding how a given culture constitutes definitions of what it means to be male or female and how, within those definitional parameters, the culture defines the kinds of characteristics, attitudes, values, behaviors, roles, and so forth that are to be understood as appropriate and inappropriate for each particular gender. According to Harding (1986), "Gender is a fundamental category within which meaning and value are assigned to everything in the world, a way of organizing human social relations" (57).

Elaborating this perspective, Flax (1987) explains that "gender can be understood only by close examination of the meanings of 'male' and 'female' and the consequences of being assigned to one or the other gender within concrete social practices" (630). Unlike other qualities (occupation, residence), gender is regarded as so fundamental to identity that it infuses every facet of individual and social life (Cirksena, 1987; Warren, 1988). Because gender is culturally defined and assigned, it is a property of social structures, beliefs, and practices, and it is on those properties that analysis must focus.

The hypothesis that socialization creates feminine gender, understood as a fundamental, pervasive aspect of identity, suggests that caring for others is central to cultural views of femininity, views that are inculcated in each new member of a society. Rosen-

blum (1989), for instance, argues that "the tenets of femininity
. . . encourage women to sacrifice for others" (200). Nancy Russo
(1981) similarly discusses the qualities of mothering as ones prescribed by the culture when she writes that within Western society
"a 'good' mother must be physically present to serve her infant's
every need . . . instantly available should her child ever need
her" (275). In each case the concrete behaviors and attitudes
women routinely demonstrate are explained as manifestations
of cultural belief systems that are inculcated as part of learning
one's gender.

Directly linking tendencies to care for others with socialized
femininity, Harding (1991) comments that "in order to make
female children feminine and womanly, parents encourage a
tendency toward concrete and relational thought and a preference for personal, caring service to other people. These traits
prepare girls and women to prefer teaching, mothering, and
other service and caring activities" (28–29). In presenting this
position, Harding insists that the traits consistently found in
women are not personal, individual ones. Rather, she insists,
"Sexism and androcentrism are culturewide social, political, and
economic characteristics, and it obscures their origins, institution-
alization, and consequences to refer to them as personal" (14).
Like others operating from a view of gender as an analytic category, Harding emphasizes structural features of society that are
embodied in individuals' concrete activities.

This form of explanation, then, assumes that socially constructed and sustained categories of gender define caring for
others as constitutive of femininity but not of masculinity. Consequently, through interaction with a variety of social institutions
that reinforce acquisition of appropriate gender role behaviors,
attitudes, and skills, women tend to develop both the capacities
and desire to care for others. Those who do not are generally
criticized for their "lack of feeling," "insensitivity to others," and
"selfishness," qualities we might note that would not lead to critical judgments of men since they are not antithetical to cultural
definitions of masculinity.

Viewed from this perspective, the activities that women and
men engage in are understood to be individual enactments of
broad social values and beliefs. In a particularly illuminating
study, Butler (1990) argues gender is not an internal quality of

individuals but rather a "performance," directed by institutions and assumptions that undergird a given society and scripted into particular discursive practices that, in turn, reinforce the existing social order. Similarly, Flax (1990) notes that what counts as "feminine" and "masculine" varies widely among cultures and within specific cultures at various times. Differences in what was required of femininity in the 1800s and today give credence to the claim that gender is socially constructed and enacted by individuals within specific, historically bound moments.

A classic in this area is Elizabeth Janeway's (1971) book, *Man's World, Woman's Place: A Study in Social Mythology*, which used the key concept of role as the starting point for analyzing Western women's patterns of attitude and activity. For Janeway, role is not a property of individuals so much as of social systems. She argues that roles are not merely individual expressions but are culturally constructed and assigned to individuals whose enactment reflects and perpetuates the values and definitions of the culture itself. In advancing this analysis, Janeway acknowledges her indebtedness to Parsons (1953), an early social theorist who observed that it is the "common culture . . . which defines, and so in one sense determines, the relative statuses of its members. . . . What persons are can be understood in terms of a set of beliefs and sentiments which defines what they *ought to be*" (18). In noting this, Parsons alerts us to the insight that cultural definitions not only influence individual development, but also serve as the basis for judging individuals' behaviors, values, and inclinations.

From Parsons's insight we can deduce the idea that cultural beliefs about what a woman ought to be form a lens through which any and all women are judged, regardless of whether they subscribe to those cultural beliefs. Gender, then, is not a quality of individuals but of the social systems they inhabit and in which they participate. Using her analysis to elaborate this basic premise, Janeway (1971) argues that through the process of socialization children learn the roles defined by their culture; in doing so, they come to understand not just prescribed activities for their roles but the meaning or value the culture assigns to those. Thus, claims Janeway, in learning one is female and in learning one is expected to care for others, a female also learns that both femininity and caring are not highly valued in Western culture.

It is at this juncture in her analysis that Janeway introduces skepticism about whether socialization adequately accounts for tendencies to care for others. If we consider only how sex roles are socialized, she suggests, we don't necessarily have to address the meanings, and specifically the values, a culture assigns to activities. From her own efforts to work with socialized gender as an explanation of women's behavioral and attitudinal patterns, Janeway discovers the limits of this view.

The question of how caring is valued in a culture, Janeway concludes, cannot be wholly explained by gender socialization alone. In reaching this judgment Janeway also suggests gender socialization cannot lead us to a full understanding of why certain people tend to care more than others. What diligent analysis of gender as an analytic category representing and expressing cultural beliefs has done is lead us to recognize the possibility that gender itself is located within larger cultural issues that must be explored to understand how gender is constructed.

Contributing to this line of thinking is Harding (1991), who recently pointed out that "gender relations in any particular historical situation are always constructed by the entire array of hierarchical social relations in which 'woman' or 'man' participates" (14). Caring, then, should be conceived as imbricated with overall attitudes and activities learned as part of acquiring gender role within a culture. Yet, this still doesn't explain why caring is generally devalued in Western culture. Even more injurious to this explanation's adequacy is its inability, by definition, to account for the existence of a tendency to care in people who are neither of female sex nor feminine gender. Illuminating this is beyond the scope of an explanation that posits socialization into gender roles as the basis of caring.

Finally, this explanation is subject to the criticism that it presupposes the very issues it's trying to explain by assuming the status and meaning of gender both exist in some reified and essentialized form and are causal of certain qualities in individuals. This formulation obscures the possibility that gender is not the cause of certain behavioral patterns but rather itself a manifestation of larger definitional practices of the culture.

So, as with the psychodynamic explanation, we see that when a socialized explanation of gender is pressed to its limits, it leaves unanswered questions. There seems to be yet a more fundamental explanation that is not fully captured in an account of care as something learned as part of gender. How, then, is gender itself socially constructed and what is the relationship between the construction of gender and caring? What if we entertain the possibility that socialization in Western societies is primarily a matter of learning about power relations and one's own position in a culture's hierarchy? This is precisely the hypothesis that has fueled much recent thought about caring.

Caring as Generated by Power Relations

A number of people studying women's identities in Western culture argue the tendency to care for others arises out of subordinate status. Tronto (1987) broaches this viewpoint in an early essay in which she argues Gilligan's view of caring is naive because it "precludes the possibility that care is an ethic created in modern society by the condition of subordination. . . . Women's different moral expression might be a function of their subordinate or tentative social position" (647, 649). Returning later to develop this idea, Tronto (1989) argues that "insofar as caring is a kind of attentiveness, it may be a reflection of a survival mechanism for women or others who are dealing with oppressive conditions. . . . Another way to understand caring is to see it as an ethic most appropriate for those in subordinate social positions" (184). The relationship between caring and subordinate status has been convincingly elaborated by others (Broughton, 1983; Henley, 1977).

Perhaps the most persuasive support for the idea that caring grows out of culturally constructed subordinate status rather than sex-role socialization would be empirical demonstration that caring is practiced by people in subordinate positions who are not female. Looking around, we find there is indeed some very intriguing evidence of precisely this. In his widely read and re-spected study *Eskimos, Chicanos, Indians*, Robert Coles (1977) finds that children of these groups (both sexes) exhibit caring for others and nature as a primary moral orientation.

Studies of black culture provide further support for the con-nection between subordinate status and caring for others. One piece of evidence comes from Gwaltney's (1980) case histories of blacks from which he concludes that blacks of both sexes are motivated by awareness of and responsiveness to others' needs and by a general understanding of themselves as interdependent with other members of their culture. Other studies of black cultures offer similar evidence that caring and a sense of connectedness to others is an important moral theme that informs the activities and attitudes of both males and females (Jackson, 1982; Nobles, 1976). Henley's (1977) influential book *Body Politics: Power, Sex, and Nonverbal Communication* is an extended demonstration that regardless of sex, individuals and groups who occupy subordinate status display a responsive orientation to others characterized by deference, attentiveness, awareness of needs, understanding of perspectives, moods and intentions, and responsiveness.

These empirical demonstrations that the tendency to care is closely aligned with subordination have been buttressed by impressive theorizing. In her far-reaching analysis of social structure and women's place within it, we've seen that Janeway (1971) considers then rejects gender—that is the socialized sex role—as a full explanation of Western women's inclination to care for others. Instead, she argues persuasively that "it comes naturally to anyone in a subordinate position. One cannot live comfortably as a subordinate (and in some extreme cases one cannot live at all) without developing a powerful sense of interpersonal relationships and social atmospherics" (112).

To illustrate this hypothesis concretely, Janeway selects one particular activity associated with caring as a focus: the desire to please others, which Gilligan and others have discussed as implicated in a tendency to care for others. Janeway's analysis merits lengthy citation:

> The whole question of pleasing is central to an analysis of woman's role . . . I am talking, of course, about pleasing as a policy . . . pleasingness as an attribute commonly expected of women and other subordinates . . . and adopted by women and other subordinates both for defense and as a means of gaining ends they cannot achieve by their own direct actions. (113)

> The powerful need not please. It is subordinates who must do so—or at least it is subordinates who are blamed if they

don't and especially subordinates who live at close quarters
with their superiors. The Negro Uncle Tom role ... the
woman's traditional role. (114)

Pleasing goes with dependence and subordination. (121)

Though among the first to suggest this interpretation of the
origin of caring, Janeway is certainly not alone in advancing it.
Bill Puka (1990) is another who has elaborated the relationship
between subordination and a tendency to care. From a careful
reexamination of the interviews on which Gilligan based her
claims, Puka derives an alternative to Gilligan's explanation that
fully accounts for her data. He suggests that "care is not a general
course of moral development, primarily, but a set of coping
strategies for dealing with sexist oppression in particular" (59).
Concurring with other critics of Gilligan in faulting her for decontextualizing care and treating it as a matter of individual
behavior, Puka hypothesizes that her approach "does not accurately identify the causes of its 'sense of service' in the sexist
nature of social institutions and sexual politics primarily" (62).

Developing the idea that the tendency to care grows out of
oppression, Puka remarks on the "uncanny relationship between
care maturity, as Gilligan portrays it, and the 'slave morality'
phenomenon long recognized" (64). Continuing this line of analysis, Puka shows how care levels described by Gilligan "bear a
strong resemblance to patterns of attitudinal assimilation and
accommodation commonly observed among poor and oppressed
groups, or in oppressive situational contexts ... ensure your
psychological survival in the face of ongoing domination [Gilli-
gan's level 1] ... play the roles those in power set for you. Serve
and sacrifice to gain their approval. . . . Be circumspect in pursu-
ing your true interests, or even in recognizing them [Gilligan's
level 2] ... ferret out spheres of power ... within the gaps of
the established power structure. Embrace the competencies of
those oppressed roles one cannot avoid [Gilligan's level 3]" (66).
For each moral stance that Gilligan explains as resulting from
feminine socialization, Puka is able to mount a persuasive competing explanation based on subordinate status.

For further support of the idea that caring is better understood as rooted in subordination than in either individual psychology or socialized gender, consider what is known about "prisoner mentality." Studies by Bettelheim (1943), Freud (1946), Sanford (1955), and Jennings, Kilkenny, & Kohlberg (1983) reveal those who are oppressed often exhibit strong tendencies to know, cater and defer to, please and identify with those in power. As a number of writers in this area have discerned, what we take to be caring may spring from quite different motives than those we tend to associate with the activity. It is certainly reasonable to acknowledge that for someone in a subordinate position, security, comfort, safety, and even survival may depend quite directly on abilities to know, interpret, please, serve, and satisfy whoever has more power. Thus, locating the genesis of caring within oppressive circumstances and subordinate position assumes considerable plausibility.

Rethinking the Origins of Tendencies to Care

So far, we have considered three different frameworks for explaining tendencies to care for others. At this point we need to be very clear about what the foregoing positions suggest as well as what they should not be interpreted to mean.

We should first note that, with the apparent exception of Gilligan, those advancing particular explanations neither ignore nor discount the veracity of other accounts. Chodorow and Miller, for example, while focusing on psychodynamic processes clearly embed their explanation within an awareness of both feminine sex roles and woman's historically low power within Western culture. Both explicitly acknowledge that to survive women must develop psychological characteristics and behavioral tendencies that please and meet the needs of those in power. Their focus on family psychodynamics, then, complements other analyses of care.

Those who emphasize sex-role socialization similarly recognize that within Western culture it is not possible to divorce gender from power since the two are associated in concrete practice, cultural beliefs, and the historical bifurcation of the society into public and private realms. Scott (1986), for instance, points to the "explicit connections between gender and power" (1072) as the basis for her argument that gender is "a primary means of signifying relationships of power. . . . Gender is one of the recurrent references by which political power has been conceived, legitimated, and criticized. . . . Gender and power construct one another" (1072–1073).[5]

Thus, the different explanations are not as much competing as they are interactive and collaborative. As we have seen, there is widely acknowledged overlap such that each is perhaps most usefully recognized as a particular point of emphasis within an overall account that recognizes caring arises out of complex interwoven processes constructed and carried out by the culture through specific socialization agencies such as families, schools, and institutions.

The account that argues oppressive conditions and/or status generate caring is perhaps the most encompassing and satisfying since it is able to subsume gender socialization and family psychodynamics. Thus, it is tempting to accept this account, at least tentatively, as the best so far articulated explanation of the conditions, personal and social positions, and cultural practices that tend to produce people who care for others.

Yet, there are reasons to resist this temptation. First, the meaning of the oppression explanation may not be as transparent as it first appears, so I want to probe it further. Second, these three formulations individually and even in combination are limited in what they can explain about caring in our culture. While each points to ways in which people are taught how to care for others, none is able to explain how meanings for care itself arise or how certain people and classes are selected to be caregivers. In the next chapter I elaborate this reservation more fully. For the moment let us simply be skeptical of the social-scientific proclivity to reduce all instances of a phenomenon to one neat category that can be explained by a single, tidy formula. Human activities are seldom that orderly, seldom that amenable to monolithic explanation. If we content ourselves with a solitary explanation, no matter how encompassing, we may sacrifice a rich understanding for the comforts of conceptual order. Such order, we might note, is often even more illusory than real.

Disturbing the Order

The original purpose in considering different explanations of
how care arises was to historicize caring in a manner that could
inform our understanding of it as a complex, situated predisposi-
tion and set of activities that arise and are enacted in particular
historical, social, personal, political, and economic contexts. Yet
the explanatory frameworks that we have considered encourage
us to sweep all manifestations of caring under one explanatory
rubric. Rather than accede to that urging, however, what seems
more useful at this juncture is to identify and embrace some of
the tensions within and among the different explanations for
the genesis of care. Out of these tensions and our refusal to
foreclose prematurely our thinking about what promotes caring
it may well be that truly provocative insights can arise.

The Cases That Don't Fit into Accounts

We might first ask whether there are cases of caring by people
who are not female and not noticeably oppressed or subordinate.
If we locate any such cases, then the comprehensiveness of proffered explanations becomes suspect. Just a little reflection will
reveal to us that subordinate status as an explanation does not
help us understand a number of instances of caring. For example,
if a tendency to care for others is rooted in subordinate status,
then how do we explain the father who sacrifices his own future
security for his child, the doctor who goes far beyond any professional obligations in showing compassion to a sick patient, the
very powerful and high status businessman who leaves his career
and commits himself personally to caring for his sick father, or
the elderly couple who are devoted to each other and daily focus
on providing assistance and comfort?

Subordination is also unable to account for instances in which
highly privileged individuals exhibit caring. Śākyamuni Buddha,
to cite a historical example, was a prince with all of the comforts
and luxuries of palatial life. Yet when he first left the protected
walls of the castle and encountered suffering in the world, he
was overwhelmed by compassion. Deeply moved, he renounced
all material comforts and devoted his life to doing what he could

to understand and ameliorate the suffering of all sentient creatures. These few examples show that even the generally robust view of subordinate status as the genesis of care is unable to give us a coherent, comprehensive explanation.

We don't want to dismiss cases that don't fit within an explanatory framework by invoking some other concept to tidy things up; for instance, we would go astray to explain away cases such as those just cited as merely instances of meeting responsibilities—paternal, professional, filial, spousal, or imperial. Likewise, we don't want to set them aside in a category of "special exceptions" to what we label the general precipitant circumstance of oppression, because to do that would be to marginalize these cases, a move that would impoverish our potential to understand the breadth of what caring may mean.

Instead, it seems more prudent to entertain the possibility that there is no single explanation of caring, no one set of circumstances that exclusively and comprehensively fosters a tendency to care for others. We can realize that subordinate status does indeed seem associated with caring without ruling out the possibility that other circumstances or influences may also encourage caring. This move deflects our attention from subordination per se and toward the kinds of practices that typically accompany it. If such practices also reside in other, nonoppressive circumstances, then perhaps we can free them from any conceptual association with subordination and examine them in their own right as clues to the genesis of tendencies to care for others.

This suggests we may find it instructive to look closely at ways that we cultivate in individuals an inclination to care for others. Our earlier consideration of socialization practices, for instance, suggests that people are taught to attend and respond to others, to think in terms of others' needs and perspectives, and to figure out what will please, comfort, and satisfy others. Inculcating abilities such as these need not be confined to contexts of oppression, nor need they be emphasized only in socializing females and subordinates. The abilities themselves and the practices that instill them, in effect, can be dissociated from any particular contexts, even ones in which they may have predominantly occurred historically. To do so also frees our understanding of what caring itself means and how it might be more generally promoted in humans.

This returns us to our earlier consideration of the concrete practices and activities that we regard as caring. If we find there are particular practices that comprise caring for others and if we can dissociate them from the oppressive circumstances in which they frequently, but not invariably, occur, then we may gain a clearer line of vision on how we might, if we choose, increase in people generally a tendency to care for others.

The Concrete Practice of Caring

Spiraling our way through our inquiry, we find ourselves back now to the question we first considered in chapter 3: what is caring, or what comprises caring? Although we have dealt with this before, it was from a different vantage point than the one we now occupy. Our examination of a primary discourse on care and our analysis of different explanations of caring should allow us to review the question with perhaps a richer appreciation of the historical, philosophical, and political undercurrents pulsing within it.

When we first tried to pin down what caring is, we specified three particular orientations as characterizing it: partiality, empathy, and desire to serve or nurture another. Perhaps we can now translate these general abilities into more concrete activities and mental proclivities that comprise caring. In turn, this would provide us with a basis for considering how to cultivate more broadly, should we choose to, those particular attitudes and skills that would lead to greater caring for others.

Responsiveness to Others

Those who have studied caring as it is enacted offer some relatively consistent observations about just what counts as caring. In his analysis of therapeutic communication, Kreps (1990) emphasizes empathy, trustworthiness, and validation or nonjudgmental acceptance of others.[6] Each of these qualities is essentially communication centered since each is displayed and perceived through interaction between people. Thus, Kreps's analysis alerts us to the importance of active responsiveness to others as essential to caring. Responsiveness, though of a more passive sort, is also central to Gilligan's (1982) discussion of caring, becoming the core of the female ethic she theorizes.

Although the language for describing the activity varies widely, responsiveness figures prominently in most accounts of caring practices (Angel, 1987; Chodorow, 1978; Miller, 1986; Noddings, 1990). Entailed in being responsive are specific abilities, including deciding to focus on another, responding to others as a means of affirming their presence and value, and listening and observing carefully in order to discern what it is that another means by her or his behaviors.

Sensitivity to Others

Kreps also finds himself in company with others studying care in stressing the importance of being sensitive to others to identify and attend to their needs, desires, perspectives, and so on. In turn, this sensitivity can be broken down into very particular activities such as paying attention to others, learning to recognize and interpret patterns in their thoughts, feelings and activities, and figuring out what their ways of indicating various things are. These activities comprise what is called "women's intuition," which Miller (1986) argues is actually a set of "skills developed through long practice, in reading many small signals, both verbal and nonverbal" (10). Responsiveness alone, then, is not enough; it must grow out of sensitivity to others' perspectives and feelings.

In discussing this kind of sensitivity to others, Janeway (1971) states that "it comes down, in the end, to an act of imagination: recognition of the reality of other people's needs" (112). Caring requires responding to another in other's terms, not one's own. This in itself is validating, to use Kreps's term, for it confirms the other's existence and importance (Wood, 1992a).

Acceptance of Others

A third theme recurrent in reports on caring is acceptance, an openness to others that allows them to feel "psychologically safe" in expressing their feelings, needs, wants, and beliefs. Long established in communication theory (Wood, 1992a) as well as in counseling practice, demonstrating a nonjudgmental regard for others is critical in creating trust and freedom sufficient to have an open relationship. Thus, actions that avoid judgment and criticism in favor of nonevaluative acceptance are ones that both communicate caring and assist in establishing a relational context that allows greater knowledge of another; in turn, these enhance the potential for yet greater responsiveness and awareness of another. Studies of comforting behaviors consistently show that affirmation is profoundly important in easing and consoling others (Burleson, 1984).

Patience

Finally, caring requires patience, a willingness to go at another's speed (Miller, 1986). The essence of patience is being willing to wait, to lay aside one's own schedule in order to accommodate others without making them feel burdensome or slow. Caring for others necessitates this kind of readiness to adjust one's own rhythm and priorities to another's, to let the other set the goals and establish what is a comfortable pace. Those who excel as mothers, nurses, and teachers, for instance, are generally known to be "interruptable." That is, they are able to put aside what they are doing in order to respond to or take care of others' needs. This kind of patience is the crux of the "good mother" concept developed by Chodorow and Miller.

Dynamic Autonomy: An Interdependent Sense of Self

These four qualities—responsiveness, sensitivity to others, acceptance, and patience—summarize a vast amount of research and observation on specific activities comprising caring. Underlying and running through all four is a larger, integrative quality that merits our attention. To be responsive, sensitive, accepting, and patient with others depends fundamentally on being able and willing to let go of, at least temporarily, preoccupation with oneself and one's own concerns. This letting go, of course, is the basis of the pervasive association of selflessness with caring, yet this may be false as an equation. While one can be selfless to the point of losing any autonomous sense of identity, this is not necessary and is certainly not ideal.

We sometimes think of self and other as opposing interests just as we may regard being connected to others as the contrast to being autonomous. Such associations, however, bespeak a limited appreciation of what autonomy means, although it is one perhaps quite widely endorsed in Western culture. In her illuminating discussion of the concept, Keller (1985) discusses dynamic autonomy as an awareness of both one's own desires, plans, motives, and viewpoints and those of others, as being comfortable thinking and acting independently and thinking and acting cooperatively or in relationship with others.

For Keller, autonomy defined by rigid separation between self and others is brittle and reflects an insecurity in one's own identity such that one cannot risk entering into another's reality for fear of losing self. The dynamic autonomy Keller recommends is fluid, secure, and able to be both with and apart from others with equal comfort and equal security in one's own selfhood. Dynamic autonomy offers us a way of understanding how a person may recognize and accommodate someone needing care without "losing self."[7] To do so requires an openness to the other, who cannot be truly understood from a removed, nonparticularized perspective. As long as a person is locked in his or her own world view, it is impossible to understand and respond to others in their own terms. One can only see and respond from the terms and vantage point of the self. Yet to care for another requires a person to suspend or at least hold apart his or her own perspective so that it isn't imposed or projected on others, and so that there is room to recognize the legitimacy of other perspectives than one's own.

Given Western culture's prevailing emphasis on self-interest and individual, independent identity, the capacity to let go of egocentrism is particularly difficult to learn and to practice. Yet without this pivotal, basic ability, it is virtually impossible to enact responsiveness, sensitivity to others, acceptance, or patience. All of the more particular qualities comprising care depend on being able to let go of one's own concerns and viewpoints, at least long enough to recognize those of another as defined by and as meaningful to that other. Perhaps the capacity to let go of self can only arise out of both security in one's own identity and a profound recognition of the interdependence of all forms of life and the ways in which each of us affects and is affected by others.

Within Western thought and conduct, such a view of self is not well developed or respected, to say the least. When we speak of "self" in Western societies we mean "the individual," the I, the autonomous agent. Yet alternate conceptions of identity do exist, some of which regard interdependence as the very essence of selfhood. For instance, the assumption that one can really develop self only by letting go of self, firmly established in Eastern culture and philosophies, remains paradoxical or nonsensical to most Westerners. It was part of the system of beliefs in Śākyamuni Buddha's home country of India, which may explain why he could feel others' suffering as his own and feel compelled to act responsively. Variable views of self highlight the need to understand how cultural definitions and the processes that create and sustain them affect our capacity to care for others in the United States.

Reframing the Question

This chapter began by exploring conditions that may foster caring for others. We now find ourselves confronting a different, more heuristic question: what has caring come to mean through its historical situation and practice in the United States? This reframing shifts our analytic focus from the origins of tendencies to care per se to the means by which caring has come to have particular meanings and to be associated with specific people. What began as an effort to adjudicate among different explanations of how care originates has evolved into a realization that any single explanation of why people care for others is both incomplete and rather beside the point. This hasn't been a wasted journey, however, because it has brought us to an important point, albeit one quite different than we initially intended.

What our analysis highlights and compels us to explore further is that care and its predominant practice by women and subordinates, like other concepts and activities of a culture, have widely accepted meanings that guide our expectations of who should care and how important caring is. The substantial observation and research informing prior explanations that locate the genesis of care in family psychodynamics, sex-role socialization, and subordination become quite helpful in revealing contexts and positions of subordination within which care and women have been situated and within which their meanings have been socially constructed and sustained. Yet these accounts do not tell us much about how those meanings are actually constructed by a culture. This issue is, in fact, beyond the explanatory scope and interest of the accounts. Existing explanations focus on how one is taught to care, not how care itself comes to have a particular meaning within a culture, an issue that may disclose why it is that certain people and not others are taught to care.

Investigation of how care itself is constituted in Western culture cannot be addressed from the frameworks we have thus far considered. To explore how a culture creates and sustains meanings to guide its activities we need to take a discursive turn— a move that will redirect our analysis, focusing it on language as primary in constructing cultural practices. As we take this turn, not only will we be seeking explanation of what is—of what meaning of care currently exist—but also we will be engaging in criticism as we ask what should be the meaning of care and how might that be cultivated in the United States.

As we move into a critical posture, we will be criticizing not just the culture "out there," but ourselves as well. *We*, after all, have created the currently prevalent low regard for caring and *we* have confined it and those who do it to the margins of our society. The critical posture toward which we now find ourselves moving also invites us to consider how we might change the historically situated but no longer functional ways in which we have constructed our attitudes and practices of caring. This line of thinking is the focus of the next chapter in which we'll consider some very realistic ways we as individuals and a collective people can reform what care means and how it is to be valued in our world.

Summary

In this chapter we have followed a winding river with many tributaries as we tried to understand the origin of tendencies to care for others. Our initial review of different explanations for caring proved less than satisfying since all explanations, albeit in quite diverse ways, reduce caring to some singular cause as if all kinds of caring are the same and all people who care for others do so from identical motives and influences. Our own consideration of caring as a set of concrete practices reveals that it is both complex and variable in practice and, presumably, in origin.

What is perhaps most important to focus on from our explorations in this chapter is the understanding that caring for others is a socially constructed idea. As such, it partakes of and furthers the ideals, goals, and beliefs of the culture in which it is situated. Caring for others, as defined in the United States, is not valuable or important; thus, it is assigned to individuals and groups whom the culture has designated as subordinate—predominantly women.

Yet life in the United States is changing. The majority of women today work and intend to keep working. Their unquestioning willingness to provide caring can no longer be assumed; their ability in terms of time and energy is also reduced as some of their vitality flows quite rightly into areas that once were closed to women. Simultaneous with this change in women's views of themselves and their goals are increasing numbers of people who require care. Babies are still being born; not as many as during the boom years nor as few as during the seventies, but many are joining us, and they require constant care. Then, too, the number of elderly people who need varying degrees of care is growing rapidly as medical and technological innovations make it possible to extend the years we can live.

Who cares? Who will care for our elders, our children, and—for that matter—any of us when we need help? Can we refashion cultural values to affirm human connections and to define caring for others as natural, important, and everyone's responsibility? Can we do so in ways that do not impose excessive losses in identity, opportunities, and status on those who provide care? It is to these questions that we turn in the next chapter.

Language is a structuring principle of society.
—C. Weedon, *Feminist Practice and Poststructuralist Theory*

Social structure is destiny.
—D. P. Moynihan, *Family and Nation*

CHAPTER 6
Taking a Discursive Turn: Constructing Care

The last chapter revealed existing accounts of caring are limited in what they can tell us. Those accounts describe how people are taught to care and they identify circumstances associated with the development of tendencies to care. What they cannot explain, however, is how the meanings for caring and women arise and are sustained in Western culture. It is to these issues that we now turn our attention. In this chapter we investigate how our culture constructs and perpetuates particular, widely shared meanings for caring and women.

My analysis builds on prior work that recognizes gender as an analytic category reflecting systematic patterns in a culture. Given this, we want first to understand the structural features of our society that establish understandings of what care is and that suggest the focus of an informed critique of its practice. This leads us to discourse, which is a primary structuring principle of our culture (Weedon, 1987, 41). We want to identify discursive practices that constitute and uphold existing structural patterns that devalue caring and associate it with women and subordinates. Understanding how discursive practices construct cultural beliefs and inform cultural practices should also illuminate means whereby we can contest the currently prevalent meanings of a social order.

113

Structuring Culture: Structuring Care

My criticisms of *In a Different Voice* center on Gilligan's disregard for ways in which society is organized such that caring is both widely devalued and assigned to women. In passing over structural considerations, Gilligan limits her vision to a description of what is and what has been the case. By this I mean that her approach decontextualizes care, removing it from complex historical, social, economic, and political contexts in which care has been practiced. Her comfort with historical views of caring and women's role in that view leaves Gilligan unable to suggest ways of changing culture itself in order to enhance caring in general.

We now depart from Gilligan and others who are basically unmindful of the social organization they describe so that we may zero in on that organization. We want to identify cultural beliefs, assumptions, and practices that mitigate against valuing care and that assign its practice to women and subordinates. This should disclose to us some of the key sites in which conventional meanings of women and care might be reconstructed.

In suggesting that the devaluation of care is structurally rooted, I am arguing that it exists in cultural patterns and institutions, not simply in individual motives and actions. A culture consists of institutions (schools, churches, business, and labor, law, and family) and practices (norms, policies, and routinized ways of doing things) that organize social life. These structuring institutions and practices are, in turn, embodied in concrete activities that simultaneously express and reinforce the overarching social organization.

Understood as specific enactments of values and understandings that reside in the larger culture, particular enactments take on significance beyond that we might ordinarily attribute to individual and group behavior. By concretely validating normative understandings of a culture, particular actions realize, that is, make "real," those abstract ideals, beliefs, and expectations. Thus, they sustain and fortify the social order from which they spring. It is for this reason that Moynihan (1986) revised Freud's famous dictum—"anatomy is destiny"—to argue that "social structure is destiny" (6). With this turn of phrase, Moynihan points out the extent to which the structure of a culture dictates the conduct and beliefs of individuals within it. Human experiences are both embodied and symbolic—simultaneously material and concrete, on the one hand, and impregnated with culturally defined meaning and placement, on the other. In this circumstance, individuals' everyday experiences at home, work, and in social situations become the sites where we concretize and reinforce those views and values that the culture has endorsed.

Chodorow (1978) pointed to awareness of social organization as prerequisite to any informed understanding of patterns in individuals and families. Embedding her analysis of women's personality development within social life as a whole, she wrote: "I argue that the contemporary reproduction of mothering occurs through social structurally induced psychological processes" (7). She then insists that "the social organization of gender is . . . a fundamental determining and constituting element of that society, socially constituted" (8).

Concurring with Chodorow, Weedon (1987) realizes the limitations of understanding or change at the "level of subjective consciousness" and, instead, insists on "stressing the importance of the material relations and practices which constitute individuals as embodied subjects . . . of the social institutions and processes which structure society" (41). Thus, to make sense of individual behaviors—for our purposes, of why and how people care—we must understand how caring is defined through the practices and institutions that comprise and structure our culture.

To begin this inquiry we may find it worthwhile to circle back on the oppression explanation to rethink what it might mean. As put forward, this explanation seems to argue that oppression tends to produce an inclination to care: thus, oppression or subordination is seen as the root "cause" of caring. It is, however, possible to derive a quite different interpretation of the research linking subordination and tendencies to care.

Assuming that social structure informs practices, we might hypothesize that it is because caring is devalued in Western culture that the activities and attitudes comprising it are taught routinely to and, thus, exhibited by those with low social status. Similarly, we can reason that because caring is defined as a personal activity within the private realm, it is inculcated into women who traditionally have been assigned to this sphere.

This revised interpretation would lead us to regard oppression and privatization as contexts rather than causes of caring. Exploring this reformulation, we see that if subordination is viewed as one circumstance associated with tendencies to care, rather than a cause of care, cultural devaluation of caring gains credibility as a primary reason that caring is assigned and taught consistently to those with subordinate status. The plausibility of this reformulation depends on a demonstration that Western culture actually does devalue caring. We would need to find convincing evidence in daily activities as well as institutional practices that care is a low social priority. So our task becomes inspecting how the structural features of our society define caring for others as well as the processes by which it persuades others to collude in and corroborate its definition. Only then may we be able to unravel the connections among caring, women, subordinate status, and cultural processes.

The Structural Devaluation of Care

Despite lip service to the contrary, there is convincing evidence that caring for others does not occupy a position of privilege in our culture's views of what is important. Miller (1986) ably articulates this overall judgment when she writes that "a society emphasizes and values some aspects of the total range of human potentials more than others, the valued aspects are associated closely with, and limited to, the dominant group's domain. Certain other elements are relegated to subordinates. Although these may be necessary parts of human experience, they are not the ones valued by that particular society. . . . American society, in the larger tradition of Western society, has valued the intellect and the executive and managerial functions" (22). Continuing with this theme, Miller points out that among the "less valued tasks" in the United States are those that "involve providing bodily needs and comforts" as well as "the realm of biology— the body, sex, and childbearing . . . interaction with children" (21–22). In short, many of the concrete activities that comprise taking care of others are defined as less valuable than tasks that assume and enhance self-interest and individual achievement.

Creating Caregivers

Once the "less valuable" tasks are specified, a society then must find ways to define some individuals or groups as responsible for doing these necessary but "trivial" activities. To do this, argues Miller, the society must label some groups as inferior in various ways and then assign to those groups whatever is shunned by those who hold power in the culture. The members of a culture who hold power reserve for themselves whatever they have defined as the "desirable and important" activities and relegate to those defined as subordinate the less desirable ones, causing Polatnick (1973) to remark with equal measures of cynicism and insight, "Men don't rear children because they don't *want* to rear children" (60). This suggests that rearing children and caring for others in general, as less desirable and valued activities, would be "logical" candidates for assignment to those designated as having subordinate status.

A complex process unfolds in order to make these designations stick to the point of being accepted as givens in the culture. Initially, there must be some rationale for assigning tasks. Usually this rationale takes the form of describing subordinates as unable to do "the more important activities" because of their putative inferiority. And, indeed, in discussions dating back to Aristotle, we find bald statements that women are inferior to men and are thus incapable of participation in the polis—the public (important) sphere of social life.

Once disqualified from the "important tasks," those designated as inferior are systematically trained to perform the "trivial" activities that are necessary but beneath those who are superior. "Inferiors" are then methodically encouraged to develop "personal psychological characteristics that are pleasing to the dominants . . . submissiveness, passivity, docility, dependency, lack of initiative" (Miller, 7). Ultimately, the process comes full circle so that the activities assigned to those whom the culture defines as inferior are regarded as less valuable *because* they are done by people of low social status: without realizing the circularity involved, we come to regard as inferior whatever is done by those we have labeled subordinate.

There is no point, of course, in trying to determine the "true"

or "intrinsic merit" of any tasks—ones valued or not valued—
for their worth is socially constructed primarily through the discursive practices of a culture. We assign what is not valuable to
those we have named as less valuable; we name as not valuable
that which is done by those who are not valuable. It's a fully
reflexive and self-reinforcing process that laces our culture at
every turn. Through this process a culture maintains roles, task
assignments, and relatively stable understandings of the meanings for various activities.

Structuring the Meaning of Care

What evidence do we have that caring is widely devalued in our
society? Perhaps the best source is not statistics or other standard
forms of proof but everyday observations and common sense
reasoning. Which lines of work are the most highly rewarded
materially and carry the greatest status in our culture? Titles
such as doctor, attorney, and CEO first spring to mind. Which
lines of work carry the least prestige and offer the most meager
material compensations? Teacher, nurse, social worker, day-care
provider, aide, nanny, maid, and janitor are certainly on this
second list. The high status professions in the United States
emphasize individual initiative and abstract activities, while lower
status is accorded to those that involve helping others in concrete,
often physical ways.

Our culture defines as menial labor those activities that assist
in keeping others and their physical contexts clean. We don't
need any formal research to convince us that our culture has
attached quite different values to conduct that is directly self-
advancing and that which focuses on helping others. It is common cultural knowledge that the so-called caring professions
are the least well paid. Harding (1991), however, makes the
interesting observation that it would be impossible for "important
people" to do their work without all of the concrete, material
assistance provided to them by "unimportant people." Reflecting
on one of Virginia Woolf's stories, Harding writes that society
"would fall apart if women did not perform day in and day out
the devalued and trivialized work that provides the social glue for
the great achievements that men in the dominant social groups
imagine they bring off all by themselves . . . that makes it possible

for elite men to spend their days contemplating 'all by them-selves'" (26).

Further evidence can be deduced by observing the machina-tions of our political institutions. Whenever Congress announces economic pressures require reductions in spending (and when, after all, is the last year this wasn't proclaimed?), the first items to be cut are those related to caring for others. Defense expendi-tures suffer a 5 percent cut while social programs for the young, the sick, and the elderly are slashed and sometimes entirely elimi-nated. NASA receives 90 percent of its former funding while a proposal to provide shelter, food, and job training to homeless citizens is scrapped. Absorbed are the expenses of redecorating politicians' offices, shabby since the last complete refurbishing was all of two years ago, but we're told we simply cannot afford to have Medicare cover the costs of home health aides for disabled and/or ill individuals with limited resources. All around there is compelling proof of not just the cultural devaluation of caring for others but the extensiveness with which that assessment is recognized and accepted by citizens.

Other evidence exists, if we require more. For instance, con-sider Kalish's (1969) conclusion from his study of death and responses to it. He found that in the United States the elderly are not generally honored, admired, or wanted and, in some cases, they receive only extremely minimal care. They are viewed as burdens whose need for solace and assistance is often, perhaps usually, resented and assigned to someone who can be hired to "take care of that." Kalish somberly concludes that within this country we don't really value our elderly, and their deaths are frequently greeted more with relief than a sense of loss and sadness.

Buttressing Kalish's disturbing report is Angel's (1987) finding that nursing homes are filled with elderly people who are fre-quently not visited by anyone, even if one or more children live nearby (40). Meanwhile, Graedon (1991), in a recent radio program, informs us that surveys reveal two trends in the United States: first, about three-fourths of the elderly who need some care prefer to live with family members; second, about three-fourths of the elderly needing care *do not* live with family mem-bers because they have not been invited.

Caring is relegated to the lower rungs of Western culture's

priorities. It is something that must be done to some minimum
degree, but it is not the kind of activity that most people in the
United States want to participate in personally. Equally important, caring is not an activity that cultural institutions and practices acknowledge and make room for in their assumptions about
people's lives. Routinely, corporations refuse to provide adequate
family leave allowances, day care for employees' dependents,
and flexible working hours so that employees can take care of
family responsibilities while maintaining their jobs.

Remember Miller's (1986) stunningly blunt observation that
"in our culture 'serving others' is for losers, it is low-level stuff"
(61). After reviewing the meager contributions to charitable
causes in this country, Rodriguez (1990) concludes Americans
try to give just enough to feel they're "good people," leading her
to comment wryly, "Give your money, salve your conscience, go
about your business. This is the practical American way" (122).
True enough, most Americans seem willing to pay, but not much,
for someone else to do the concrete caring they choose not to
do since they have to go on about their more important, more
valuable, more self-centered and self-advancing business.

Coming back now to our effort to rethink the findings that
link oppression with tendencies to care, we find the question has
shifted somewhat, as has our effort to answer it. The evidence
that caring is devalued in U.S. culture is overwhelming and pervasive. Given this, there is basis for reinterpreting conventional
analyses of the linkage of oppression and caring, which implied
that oppression "causes" caring. The alternate reading, which
we have now seen is consistent with the personal and institutional
practices that structure our culture, holds that because caring
itself is devalued, it is assigned to those who are defined as having
subordinate status.

It appears, then, that the conclusion usually drawn by those
advancing the subordination explanation may be the victim of
the well-known fallacy that equates correlation with causation.
Our analysis reveals it is equally plausible, if not more so, to
believe that cultural practices, both material and symbolic, construct subordination and a view of caring for others as one of
the lesser tasks in our culture. Thus, it may well be the definitional
processes of our culture that link caring with subordination by

assigning it and other devalued activities to those it has defined as inferior.

This reconfiguration of the association between oppressive conditions and tendencies to care not only changes our understanding of what care is, but also it moves us away from a monolithic explanation that reduces all acts of caring to a singular cause. If the devaluation of care is structurally produced as I have suggested, then it is possible to inquire further into the cultural meanings associated with caring and caregivers.

The low status of caring in Western culture is cemented by its historical location in the private sphere, which at least since the Industrial Revolution has been regarded as the realm of activities less important to social life than those of the public sphere. Associated with the devalued private sphere, caring and caregivers have been relegated to the margins of cultural life. Because caring historically has been predominantly enacted by women and has been associated with the lesser-valued private domain, the concept of caring itself is now defined as peripheral to the "significant concerns" of the public culture.

Discourse carried out in the curbstones and corners of the culture reflects and reinforces the association among caring, women, the private sphere, and subordinate status, and thereby sustains a systemic devaluation of caring. Because women, too, historically have occupied lower positions in social life, they are associated with subordination and caring in ways that are constantly recreated through a variety of cultural and familial processes. Riddling the history of cultural practice in the United States are these associations that interact with each other to buttress beliefs and assumptions that constitute our social order.

Grounding the value of caring in the structural features of a culture seems to advance our understanding of caring in ways that prior formulations could not. Attention to social structure reveals how social organization itself is produced, that is, how the values and assumptions comprising a social order are entrenched through concrete practices and policies. Further, it shows what is required in terms of institutional life and practices to maintain a given set of social arrangements. A structural account, then, appears to move beyond the previously advanced ones in its ability to account for the very organization that is reinforced and passed on within familial and other contexts of socialization. Structural understanding seems able to elucidate the nature of the hegemonic order and how it sustains itself by specifying the assignments of roles and particular tasks that embody and, thereby, perpetuate its organization. This perspective is also heuristic since it prompts us to ask further questions, questions that burrow more deeply into the structuring principles of society by asking how those principles are themselves constructed.

A culture is structured to reproduce itself systematically. Were this not true, a culture could not endure. What must be reproduced for a culture to survive is its social organization, consisting of institutional life, normalized practices, and particular hierarchies that define the value of the array of people and activities that make up cultural life. These structural features or social organization, however, must be understood as what Marx labeled "suprastructure." In using this term Marx was pointing out that understanding how a society is organized does not in itself account for how it persists. Some more fundamental force must be disclosed to account for the persistence of social orders.

We are trying here to locate what gives rise to the surface level aspects of social organization that we can observe and whose implications we can trace: the concrete institutions, beliefs, practices, and ways of doing things that constitute social life must themselves be constituted somehow. How that happens, I argue, is through discourse—the range of symbolic activities by which members of a culture name, legitimize, and establish meanings for social organization.

The Discursive Turn

In our effort to go beyond explaining how social values are reproduced and inquire into how they are produced, we have noted already that institutions and practices comprising social organization work to maintain the existing order by concretizing its constituent assumptions over and over again in daily activities. Building on this, we turn now to the underlying issue of how social organization itself is brought into being, especially how equations of caring with femininity, subordination, and the private sphere are constructed and sustained such that they are passed without question from one generation to the next.

In making a discursive turn we center our attention on the symbolic activities whereby humans define their worlds and the people and activities within them. The generative basis of social organization is discourse, through which we articulate and justify particular understandings and meanings that guide and structure activities throughout a society. The power of discourse in cultural life has been recognized since the time of Plato and Aristotle. Yet, richly layered understandings of discourse as a primary agency for constituting both society and the individual have not been with us for so long.

In his still influential work at the University of Chicago in the early part of this century, George Herbert Mead (1934) identified language as the critical means whereby "society gets into the individual." Mead was among the first to recognize clearly that we are "talked into humanity," that is, through interacting symbolically with others we learn not only the language of our culture but more importantly the assumptions and values inherent in that language.

For Mead, the self is not a birthright but something that is acquired—can *only* be acquired—through interacting symbolically with others. Thus, insisted Mead, it is through discursive interactions that a person is taught what means what in her or his culture, an understanding that enables the individual to participate competently in the culture and, in so doing, to reinforce the very meanings learned in the process of acquiring symbolic consciousness and cultural membership.

Mead's heuristic insights have been extended and refined by a number of subsequent theories of language as constitutive of social life. The formative work of Saussure (1974), among others (Derrida, 1973, 1976; Foucault, 1973; Kristeva, 1981; Lacan, 1977; Moi, 1986), demonstrates the power of language to constitute our understandings of the world. Language is understood to be not merely an instrument by which pregiven realities are described, but a generative agency that actually constructs our understanding of what is. This is to say, language defines what experiences are and, inherently, what they mean. Weedon concisely clarifies this distinction by noting that "meaning is produced within language rather than reflected by language" (23). From this perspective, efforts to understand how social organization comes into being, as well as how a given organization might be contested, focus on language as the principle means by which a social order is established and made meaningful to those who will participate in it.

Recognizing the constructed nature of social organization, however, in no way implies it is somehow "less real" or it doesn't have material effects on individuals. The symbolically constituted world in which we live has very real consequences for individuals' beliefs, activities, options, and subjective identities. The definitional processes of the society into which we are born in fundamental ways establish the limits of how we can see ourselves and what we conceive as plausible ways of acting in the world. As phenomena are named, evaluated, and linked with other phenomena, we form expectations of what is normal, appropriate, or even possible in terms of identity, activities, and beliefs; these expectations, in turn, guide the concrete activities of our daily lives. As children, in the normal process of socialization, learn language, they import preestablished-established social meanings and then use those to define, direct, and evaluate their own activities as well as those of others (Mead, 1934).

This view of language is sometimes misrepresented as an argument that there is no "real reality." Understanding the formative power of language, however, does not require assuming there is no empirical world. Instead, this perspective simply assumes that the meaning or significance of the experiences and ideas is neither absolute nor given. Because social values inhere in symbols, children, in acquiring language, simultaneously inherit the values and assumptions of the social order into which they are born.

The power of language is to name and evaluate concrete realities as well as abstract concepts so that they assume salience and meaning for us. Naming is a critically important symbolic activity, for in naming we extract from the buzzing confusion of the world only certain things for notice. When we name something we call it to our attention and, thereby, imbue it with a prominence not conferred upon all the rest of the buzzing confusion we neglect to name. The rest of that buzzing world may still "be there" in some sense, but it does not assume salience in our reflective consciousness because it remains unnamed and, therefore, largely unnoticed.

The importance of naming for consciousness is evident in the common experience of taking a class in winetasting. Presumably a person who would take such a class has previously tasted wine, so wines exist as empirical realities. In the class, however, the instructor makes distinctions in qualities of wine that had heretofore escaped the notice of our budding oenophile. As the instructor points out *bouquet, length, finesse,* and *subtlety,* our student begins to recognize—to notice—these qualities; once they are called to attention, in fact, the student can no longer not notice them. In naming these, the instructor makes them objects of attention and consciousness, and they become part of how the neophyte now experiences wine—part of what wine now means.

The process of naming is, of course, far from neutral. Whatever language we use connotes particular evaluations of what it is we name. For instance, the "bouquet" of a good pouilly-fuissé is something different than the "smell" of an overage burgundy. Of course, how we use language to name and establish value is frequently of greater consequence than merely affecting our responses to wines. Recent cultural practice offers two particularly significant examples of how naming shapes meaning. Twenty years ago the terms *date rape* and *sexual harassment* were not in use. They have now been named into existence and are widely, albeit not yet universally, recognized in ways they were not in decades past.

Doubtless many women in the sixties were coerced into sexual intercourse by their dates. However, because this had not been labeled rape, it tended to be defined by women as "He went too far" or even "I guess maybe I 'asked for it' by letting him kiss me." Inventing the term *date rape* named as criminal any forced sexual activity, regardless of whether it is inflicted by a date or a stranger. The existing meanings for *rape* are carried forward into the term *date rape,* which is defined as no less immoral and illegal because it is instigated by someone the victim knows and perhaps responded to with a degree of affection at other times. In naming as rape any instance of forced sexual intercourse, regardless of a preexisting relationship, we place the activity within the category of crimes, rather than in its former, more innocent category of dating conduct, albeit extreme and unpardonable. A new name thus creates a new meaning.

A similar process of redefining long-standing behaviors can be seen in the last few years' efforts to name and elevate to consciousness various kinds of sexual harassment, generally, though not exclusively, perpetrated against women (Wood, 1992b). When I attended college some twenty years ago, I heard stories of professors who made advances to my dormmates, and I twice experienced this myself. In every case we—like hundreds of other women—felt guilty rather than outraged, faulted ourselves for somehow provoking the assault rather than blaming the faculty who violated our rights and the bond of trust between professors and students, and regarded the incidents as just one more problem women had to tolerate rather than as something we had a right to protest.

During the past five years, sexual harassment has been named, has been made salient in public consciousness, and has been defined as "unacceptable" and "prosecutable." From legal actions brought against companies by employees who were harassed to informal mediations and disciplinary measures in various institutions to the much-publicized Hill-Thomas hearings in the fall of 1991, we see firm evidence that a practice long in existence can be renamed in ways that change what it means and, thus, its pragmatic implications. These examples highlight the power of discourse to construct understandings of particular activities and ourselves. Equally important, they illuminate the promise of discourse as a means to change what things mean within a culture. This is to say, then, that just as discourse formed the understandings we have, we can also use discourse to reform those understandings.

Among the understandings in Western culture, three are especially pertinent to our inquiry: the entrenched division between the public sphere of productive labor and the private sphere of reproductive labor (Chodorow, 1978, 5–8; Cohen, 1991; Parsons, 1949/1964); the association of caring with women and womanliness; and the subordination in importance of caring activities to more instrumental, self-interested pursuits. These, along with other understandings comprising the prevailing ethos of Western culture, are constituted through discursive interactions occurring at various sites within the culture.

It may prove useful here to consider some concrete examples of how the existence and value of particular activities pertinent to caring and women are actually constituted in particular discursive sites. Political chambers are one important discursive arena

within which specific activities are recognized and their importance is established and announced: as congressional representa-
tives reduce tax credits for children while increasing tax write-
offs for corporations, they name business activities more important and more worthy of support than childrearing. When
President Bush vetoed the family leave bill, he defined family
responsibilities as matters businesses need not accommodate and
defines caring for families as outside the purview of government
action. When substantially greater funds are allocated for research on prostate cancer than breast and cervical cancer, which
have been shown to affect more people, the survival of men is
named as more important than that of women.

     Another discursive site is corporations and businesses: in estab-
lishing maternity leaves but not paternity or parental leaves,
women are named as those who do and should take care of
children; by not being named, fathers are defined as not being
primary caregivers (Cornell, 1991; Mann, 1989). Of this practice,
Weedon (1987) observes, "It is difficult . . . for men to play a
full role in child care when they are not entitled to parental
leave" (2). Labeling child care as a "woman's issue" similarly
situates raising children within the private sphere, which has
long been regarded as "woman's domain." As long as this label
is used, how we care for our children will not be seen as a concern
of men, much less of the polity in general (Cohen, 1991; Cornell,
1991; Friedan, 1981; Hewlett, 1991). Similarly, when corporations and industry name only maternity leaves or even parental
leaves, but not family leaves, they include newborn or newly
adopted children within the compass of those as worthy of care
but exclude older children and spouses, elderly family members,
and ill or disabled relatives.

     There are other ways in which business and labor act as a
discursive site for defining the place and role of women and, by
implication, men. In 1989, Schwartz gave a name to a long-
standing informal practice whereby organizations define female
employees who have children as "not serious professionals." Creating "the mommy track" for these women, Schwartz proposes
that working women be separated into two groups: career-pri-
mary women, who would get the kinds of training and opportunities necessary for advancement, and career and family women,
who would get neither (Schwartz, 1989). Such a practice would,

as critics quickly pointed out (Cornell, 1991; Mann, 1989), per-petuate two assumptions that have consistently disadvantaged working women: First, it would define having children as an impediment to professionalism for women but not for men. Sec-ond, in the unsurprising absence of any parallel proposal for a "daddy track," it would fortify the "imposed convention that mothers are the primary caretakers of children" (Cornell, 404).

A third discursive site that riddles our lives at every turn is the media, which frequently not only perpetuate women's subor-dinate status in the society, but also encourage women to accept that position. We've already considered how one book, Gilligan's *In a Different Voice*, invites women to accept their traditional role as caregivers. Other examples abound.

Perhaps one of the most dramatic demonstrations is advice given to women who appeal to agony columnists in popular women's magazines. Weedon (1987) reports that the typical ad-vice offered "urges women to make the best of oppressive struc-tures of family life. As wives and mothers, we are encouraged to accommodate ourselves to families at the expense of our own feelings and the quality of our lives. Examples of this can be found in the advice columns of all popular women's magazines" (38). Here we see another concrete expression of pervasive dis-cursive practices that legitimize and reinforce particular beliefs about "woman's place" and "woman's role." We can also see the profound significance of understanding that experience is fundamentally discursive in how it is constructed and what it means.

Punctuating culture at every turn are discursive interactions—formal and informal, public and private, obvious and subtle—that name and legitimate certain practices and ideologies and, simultaneously, do not name others—do not bestow symbolic existence on them. Thus, when discourse is broadly understood as symbolic practices it emerges as a primary means whereby a culture defines and sustains its structure and, with that, the tangi-ble activities that individuals enact in their daily lives. Discourse, then, can be regarded as "the structuring principle of society" (Weedon, 41), because it is through the symbolic structuring of experience that we arrive at understandings of what social life is and what that implies for our own expectations, possibilities, and activities. It is also through our own discursive participation in social life that we reinforce or contest the resident meanings of our culture.

The discursive turn we have made here now allows us to reinterpret the explanations for care that have been advanced by positioning them in relation to the generative agency of discourse. Rather than invalidating them, our analysis informs us of *how* to look at them. Reconsidering these explanations through the lens established in this chapter suggests we may understand family psychodynamics and gender role socialization as critical processes whereby a culture reproduces the social organization that has been discursively constituted, legitimated, and sustained.

Socialization into male and female gender roles, including importantly understanding the activities and nonequivalent value attached to each, occurs in the broad, pervasive contexts of the culture (schools, media, legal systems, churches, business, and labor). The family, by contrast, is a highly personal site within which individualized attention can be given to inculcating the established social organization and its incumbent roles. The personal socialization that transpires in the "private sphere" works in concert with more pervasive, less personalized forces in the larger society to reproduce the understandings of social life that have been constructed and upon which the endurance of the culture in its present form is predicated. Thus, society is organized to ensure that the cultural ideology is passed on as one generation's legacy to the next: it is a crucial inheritance if the existing social order is to be sustained.

In the ongoing conversation that constitutes a culture, we name and give meaning to the host of activities and ideals that comprise our social organization. Through processes that begin at birth and continue throughout each person's life, the discursively constructed organization is constantly, relentlessly, unendingly concretized and normalized so that it becomes for all of us the "taken-for-granted."

Yet our understanding of how cultural practices create and sustain associations among women, the private sphere, subordination, and caring need not be fatalistic, leading us inevitably to conclude the force and pervasiveness of these practices ensure continuity of the existing social order. With recognition of the generative nature of discourse comes empowerment—the ability to use discourse strategically to change the historically situated but no longer functional ways in which we have constructed our attitudes and practices of caring.

Discourse, then, becomes pivotal in any efforts we might undertake to alter the ways in which caring for others is defined, assigned, and valued in our culture. Using discourse to change social meanings is precisely Poster's (1989) point when he celebrates the critical tendency, which "insists that what is can be disassembled and improved considerably." He argues for the importance of resisting "the inscription on the face of social practices which says 'Do not tamper with me for I am good, just, and eternal'" (3). In the next chapter we pursue Poster's invitation.

To consider ways to revise embedded associations and assumptions that guide, or misguide, our conduct is to embrace our responsibilities as creators, not merely recipients of a culture. Our task now is to ask how we might create and participate in cultural practices and processes capable of advancing enriched understandings of self, others, and human connectedness, understandings that might, in turn, cultivate meanings for caring that depart from those currently prevalent in the United States.

Language is the place where actual and possible forms of social organization and their likely social and political consequences are defined and contested. Yet it is also the place where our own sense of ourselves . . . is constructed.

—C. Weedon, *Feminist Practice and Poststructuralist Theory*

CHAPTER 7
At a Cultural Crossroad: The Future of Care in the United States

Baking bread, weaving cloth, and taking care of children are sacred acts to us. Cooking and cleaning too are valued, for upon these tasks depend the health and comfort of us all. And in this society we honor our elders by spending time with them and learning from them and making them more comfortable. We care for them as well as those who are sick, and we do so with a pleasure and satisfaction born of our belief that all life is good and so anything that sustains and enhances life is also good. Here we all recognize that nourishing life in its many forms is central for we know that no one of us is truly separate from all others—our lives are interwoven. This is the secret of life.

In our small society cooperation among all members is essential. We do not differentiate tasks and people; instead, we all participate in all activities that we as a group need to survive. For instance, both women and men in our culture hunt and gather. Both take care of the young. Grandmothers and grandfathers alike look after our children, sometimes for long periods when both parents are out hunting game or gathering vegetation for all of us to eat. From an early age, our children participate with us and, like us, they engage in the whole range of activities needed for our health and comfort. They hunt with us and assist in cleaning and

cooking and in caring for family and all members of our
group. Interdependence is a way of life for us: it is the only
way to survive.

No, the above paragraphs are not misprints or printer's errors.
Nor are they science fiction. Rather, they are descriptions. The
first account summarizes Eisler's (1987) study of neolithic societies; the second is from Van Leeuwen's (1990) report on a pygmy
society she observed at length. Many cultures, different in time
and place from our own, structure their social order by beliefs
that emphasize reverence for life and interdependence. These
beliefs, in turn, lead to specific cultural practices, including defining as centrally important all activities related to the preserva-
tion and enhancement of life.

Unlike our own culture, in some neolithic societies and in a
number of contemporary Eastern cultures caring for others and
enhancing life itself are considered highly valuable activities, ones
reinforced by a whole array of cultural processes and practices.
Nurturing others and, more generally, supporting life, including
nature, are not relegated to citizens of lower status or caste. All
members of the culture—men and women, children and adults,
privileged and nonprivileged alike—respect nurturing and caring, and all participate in these activities.

My purpose in opening with these two stories is to dramatize
the generally recognized point that cultural values are arbitrary.
While the organization of our culture seems somehow "natural"
or "right," it is actually only one of many possible organizations.
That it has come to seem right and natural results from our
familiarity with it and the array of practices that reinforce this
as *the* way we live. Janeway (1971) emphasizes this when she
writes that "the social world that we share with others is a world
we have imagined together and agreed to believe in" (139). The
import of Janeway's insight is that the social world is constructed.
As chapter 6 argued, it is through our activities that we create
assumptions, values, and ways of doing things that we come to
regard as "right" and "natural."

If our social world is created, then it follows that it can be
recreated, reformed, and redefined by us. And Weedon, quoted
at the outset of this chapter, points to discourse as a primary
agency whereby we construct and reconstruct our social order

and, with it, of ourselves. Since we do define what our culture is—since we, in fact, cannot avoid doing so—it is important for us to reflect on the values and goals we really want to direct our lives. Taking a cue from Janeway, we begin by asking what kind of a world we want to imagine together, what kind of a world we want to agree with each other to believe in.

This chapter considers how we might transform our culture's understandings of caring, and, thus, the kinds of lives we lead. Thus, this chapter aims to explore how we might put into practice the understandings of discourse and social organization developed in prior chapters. To begin, we look at the tensions that arise from structural constraints our current social organization imposes on meeting needs for care. Identifying social, political, pragmatic, and personal ways in which prevailing social arrangements inhibit our ability to care for others should suggest some avenues for change; it should point us toward ways to contest and redefine cultural practices so that we are able to care for others without excessive costs to ourselves. This will lead us quite naturally to consider how we might redefine what care itself means and who should be concerned about it. Throughout this discussion we will also be considering how we might persuasively weave revised definitions into the tapestry of social life.

We need to address these issues with all of the energy and ingenuity we can muster since the health and, perhaps, the very survival of our culture are at stake. Our quest is to generate cultural beliefs and practices that would make caring more honored and more possible than it currently is.

The Crisis of Care in the United States

While I was writing this book, The National Commission on Children, a bipartisan group appointed by Presidents Reagan and Bush and Congress, issued a devastating report. The prestigious panel recommended an extensive package of proposals, most unanimously supported by liberal and conservative members alike, to address what it labeled the crisis facing America's children. According to the commission, the future of our country is in jeopardy because we are not caring adequately for our children. Ranging from government programs to provide universal health insurance for pregnant women, tax credits, and

childcare to greater parental involvement, the commission sig-
naled an alarm that America's children are at risk and that we
must take substantial action soon if they and we are to have
promising future. If all of the commission's proposals were enacted the cost would just exceed fifty billion dollars annually. Is
this too much to spend on improving the physical, mental, and
spiritual health of our children? Compare this price tag to the
two billion dollars the United States spends on a single B-2
bomber. Two billion dollars would fund over four hundred new
elementary schools or textbooks for more than sixteen million
students (Anderson, 1991). In the contrast between our culture's
willingness to spend two billion dollars on one military plane and
its reluctance to invest in its children lies a profound statement
about our national priorities. Unless providing care and enabling
individuals to engage in caring becomes a higher priority than
it has been, all of us—not just our children—are at risk.

The crisis of care in the United States is pervasive. A broad
range of human needs goes unmet because of impediments that
constrain our ability to care for others. Let's consider further the
problems attendant in raising children, perhaps the prototypical
care relationship. Concerned that there is only an illusion of
choice in women's lives, Friedan (1981) asks how a woman can
freely choose to have and nurture a child "when her job isn't
geared to taking care of a child, when there is no national policy
for parental leave, and no assurance her job will be waiting for
her if she takes time off to have a child" (23). In 1986 Hewlett
was still asking the same question, which led her to investigate
and, ultimately, to indict America's lack of support for childrearing. Lack of substantial changes impelled Hewlett to write a
second, more urgent book in 1991 in which she reiterates the
precarious plight of many families in our country.

The question is central to the crisis of care in the United States.
As women's roles have changed, they have entered the workforce
in enormous numbers, come to depend on their salaries for
economic security, learned the satisfaction of being recognized
and rewarded for skills, and enjoyed the stimulation of working
outside of the home. There is, as Friedan says, "no going back.
The women's movement was necessary. But the liberation that
began with the women's movement isn't finished. The equality
we fought for isn't livable, isn't workable, isn't comfortable" (40).

It is this lack of workability that constitutes what Friedan calls "the second stage" of feminism which grows out of changes in attitudes and roles wrought in the 1960s.

The greater, though still inadequate, equality in work and civic life isn't livable largely because it hasn't been paralleled by sufficient equality in domestic life. Friedan reports that "after nearly twenty years of the women's movement, it becomes clear that most women are still saddled with the work they used to do in the family . . . in addition to the hard new 'male jobs'" (83). Chodorow's (1978) prophetic statement, issued fourteen years ago, has become a reality: "Fundamental changes in the social relations of production do not assure concomitant changes in the domestic relations of reproduction" (6).

Pointing to the impossibility of simultaneously being fully involved in a career and raising a child, Hewlett (1986) reports that many women find the still prevalent "rigid standards of the 1950s 'cult of motherhood' are impossible to combine with the equally rigid standards of our fiercely competitive workplaces" (15–16). And the majority of working women today do not find their husbands are willing to share equally in the responsibilities of home life. Hochschild's findings on this are unambiguous: only 20 percent of the husbands in two-worker families share equally in the work of raising children and taking care of the home. Okin (1989) concurs that men and women sharing the responsibilities of home and family simply has not happened.

Yet, caring for children is not the only urgency facing us as a culture. *Newsweek* (Beck et al., 1990) tells us that taking care of a dependent adult has become a second full-time job for many women (46). More accurately *Newsweek* might have called this a third full-time job, since many women who care for aged parents are also providing the primary care for their children. It appears that what the commission labeled the "crisis in childcare" is paralleled by a crisis in elderly care.

Substantial changes in demographics as well as occupational patterns render the traditional system of taking care of elderly ineffectual. Medical advances have greatly extended the lives of Americans so that more people are living to older ages: there simply are more elderly now than in former eras. Compounding this is the relatively fewer number of working people to support elderly citizens: whereas there were twenty working people for each elderly person at the turn of this century, by the year 2000 there will be only two working adults for each older person. And only one of them—the woman—will be pulling double or triple shifts.

A primary reason greater domestic equity has not come about is that we have not abandoned, or even materially modified, traditional assumptions about men's and women's "proper" roles. While our views of the public world have begun to reflect women's presence, our ideas about the private world of the home have not evolved substantially. Specifically, there has been no significant departure from the expectation that women will be the primary caregivers. Unshaken by numerous changes in public and work life, belief in women's primary responsibilities for home, family, and caring remains relatively resolute.

From her analysis of cultural mythologies, Janeway (1971) offers this explanation for the lack of change in views of the home as "woman's sphere": "Even when there is large agreement that women have a perfect right to work if they want to, as there is today, the effort to change customs and institutions may lag very considerably because of the mythic residue at the bottom of our minds" (191). In other words, Americans tend to find it acceptable, in some cases desirable, for women to work as long as and only as long as they still meet all of their traditional responsibilities in caring for their homes and families.[1] The right that women have won seems to be the right to work twice or even three times as hard as they once did, doing their old job plus a new full-time job. This is hardly a satisfying triumph. Even if it were, Hochschild (1989) tells us, women working the double shift would be too tired to celebrate the victory.

Whatever adjustments have been made in response to women's increasing participation in work has been almost entirely on the part and at the expense of women. According to Friedan (1981), "Professions and careers are still structured in terms of the lives of men whose wives took care of the parenting and other details of life" (87). Any person who wants to hold a job and to advance is expected to be first and foremost a worker, not a member of a family. Yet, nearly two-thirds of families today have no full-time homemaker to take care of all of those family matters that were once managed for the partner who worked outside of the home. The conflicting expectations of the work front and home-front can be devastating for women, families, and—ultimately—the society (Hewlett, 1991; Kanter, 1977; Wood & Conrad, 1983). Persisting belief in women's responsibilities for caring sustains recalcitrance to change social arrangements to accommodate family and work issues of the 1990s. "If society assumes implicitly that women shouldn't work because their place is in the home," notes Janeway, "then there is no need for society to do anything to help them out. No need for day nurseries or nursery schools or public health nurses who can come in when a child is sick" (190). Despite major changes, U.S. businesses and government, for the most part, cling to old assumptions, traditional policies, and intractable views of professionalism that are inappropriate for employees, who lead different lives and have different needs than those for whom the assumptions, policies, and standards were designed.

Consider a concrete example of unrealistic practices that reflect failure to adapt to the presence of women in the workforce. Even in 1990, reports Deborah Rhode, "few American companies have provided paternity or parental leave policies" (1990b, 210). Those organizations that have acknowledged newborns' need for constant care may require time off for a worker have largely restricted their "solutions" to maternity leaves. Yet because there is no consistent national policy, leaves vary from a few weeks to a year, from paid to unpaid, from guaranteeing a position will be held open to providing no assurance whatsoever.

Even when institutions claim to offer paid maternity leave, there are often hidden penalty clauses for any woman who avails herself of this benefit. For instance, in many companies taking maternity leave is interpreted as evidence that a worker is not career-oriented, and she is taken off of any fast track for advance-ment and opportunity (Schwartz, 1989). Or consider the policy at several universities: a woman may take maternity leave (usually called "disability") with full salary, but the unarticulated cost—the penalty clause—is that no funds are provided to hire a re-placement to teach the absent professor's classes. The de facto "solution" is assigning colleagues to cover her classes as overloads for which they are not compensated, a system guaranteed to create resentment and ill-will toward women who take leaves.

Not Just a "Women's Issue"

Yet, this is not properly cast as "a woman's problem" or a "women's issue." It is clearly a problem for whole families. Contemporary constraints on caring well for children and others involve and deeply affect all members of families. Women in particular and families in general are stretched to the breaking point to fulfill responsibilities outside of the home while also sustaining some level of quality in family relationships (Beck et al., 1990; Hewlett, 1991; Hochschild, 1989; Wood, 1986).

All members of families are potential victims of the strains created by substantial and frequently conflicting expectations of home and work. Many women who juggle the unrelenting and inflexible demands of work along with the unremitting needs of families report being fatigued to a point of jeopardizing their health (Hochschild, 1989). Children miss knowing there is someone who will be there for them when they have needs, including the ongoing, nonemergency need for companionship and engagement with parents (Friedan, 1981; Hewlett, 1986, 1991; Hochschild, 1989; Okin, 1989). In too many cases children and adolescents today interact more with computers than on-the-go, overcommitted parents. Some husbands resent their wives' reduced devotion to home, family, and intimacy (Hochschild, 1989). Parents and in-laws often feel neglected by adult children, who have no room in their lives and no time in their schedules to help or even visit them. And many wives feel guilty about not meeting the collage of expectations others have of them (Berg, 1986) and resentful themselves at the expectation that they will pull triple shifts and will always, always be on call for everyone (Halpern, 1987; Hochschild, 1989; Miller, 1986; Okin, 1989). Everyone involved is strained by current social arrangements.

Another reason not to configure the problem of who cares as a "woman's issue" is that traditional parenting practices deprive both male and female children of important benefits. As Okin (1989) points out, more equitable parental roles promote more just families and, thus, contexts in which children may develop a sense of justice (185). Further, Chodorow (1978) convincingly argues that a system in which women are primary or exclusive caregivers and fathers are largely absent produces "assymetries [*sic*] in the relational experiences of girls and boys, which account for crucial differences in feminine and masculine personality" such that females have difficulties maintaining separation from others and males have difficulties achieving connection (169). Obviously, neither of these difficulties is desirable; more important, they are not inevitable.

Chodorow urges changes in parenting practices to enable boys and girls to emerge from childhood more whole, more able to both make connections and retain autonomy. Concurring opinions come from most who have studied children's development, including Eichenbaum and Orbach (1983b) who state flatly that "we certainly have enough information to tell us that both women and men suffer under the present constructions. As social beings we will create new ways of childrearing" (183). In concluding their work, these clinicians argue more equal parenting is needed if "there is to be a change in the psychologies of the coming generations of girls and boys. A new balance must be created in which both women and men participate in the world outside of the home as well as the world inside of the home" (201).

A less conspicuous and potentially more damaging consequence of these strains is becoming further separated from the very pulse of life. Nurturing families and making a home, which can be intrinsically gratifying, too frequently now are regarded as chores to be accomplished as efficiently as possible in order to get on to the next task that must be done. Sacrificing mindful participation in generative processes for an instrumental focus on results is an exchange that jeopardizes our capacity to notice and participate in rhythms of life (Nhat Hanh, 1988).

All members of families are potentially affected by the double whammy of cultural values that assume a woman will care for others and business practices that demand she give full, undivided attention to her job. Likewise, all members of families are caught in the bind that comes from living a life markedly different from prior times within a public sphere that acts as if nothing has changed and, thus, does not substantially moderate its demands. Only at peril do we ignore the unqualified conclusion of the 1991 Report of the National Commission on Children: in the United States many families have reached or exceeded a breaking point. The strains are unmanageable and unacceptable.

Not Just a Family Issue

Yet, even defining this as a family problem is likely to mislead us since it involves more than families. Both individuals and families live in a culture that defines acceptable roles, values, and codes of conduct. Thus, the extent to which our society enables, or fails to enable, people to work and take care of families will influence the nature of America in the future. The argument is really very simple: families not only, affect the society, they are the society. The ways in which parents raise children and care for elderly members, for instance, have profound significance for the culture since their children and elderly, with their attitudes, tendencies, and—in some cases—problems, become part of the whole and affect us all. Stresses, strains, and pressures that lace contemporary families often lead to marital discord or dissolution, problems with children's involvement in school and recreational activities, and necessarily, inevitably distractions from work. The repercussions of strains within families reverberate throughout society, taking a steady, relentless toll on all who comprise it.

Resolving the strains and pressures confronting families today clearly exceeds the limited material and personal resources that specific families can bring to bear. It is inarguably a cultural concern. On this point Rhode (1990b) is insistent: "The issue is not simply how well society accommodates women's particular biological capacities, but how highly it values intimate human relationships and the care related obligations that such relationships impose" (211). Creating equitable ways to care for others is a cultural priority, a social issue.

Regardless of whether we individually face problems in and between our work and family lives, we are all—each and every one of us—implicated in the problems as well as in figuring out better ways of living for all of us. Industry, government, education, civic and social organizations, individuals, and communities have reason to work together to find new ways of defining life and work so that we can be responsibly involved in both by building families that are just and loving, which, in turn, create a society that is vibrant and compassionate.

The kinds of problems we have identified have been (mis)cast too often as issues in the private sphere that are the responsibility of individuals and families. Invoking the principles of privacy and minimum interference in private life, the government has been largely unresponsive to problems that families face as a result of the social organization in America (Jones, 1988). Daniel Patrick Moynihan (1986) indicts governmental policies for their nearly exclusive focus on "the individual, and only in the rarest circumstances [defining] the family as a relevant unit." He goes on to point out that this pattern is "almost uniquely American. Most of the industrialized democracies of the world have adopted a wide range of social programs designed specifically to support the stability and viability of the family" (4).

Hewlett (1986) concurs. From her cross-cultural study of how children and families are provided for, Hewlett found "most advanced industrial countries . . . have made considerable progress toward providing public or publicly funded child care. . . . Only America is decreasing public support for children" (129). Small wonder, given this, that the National Commission reports our children are in jeopardy and will remain so unless we name as a public issue the ensuring that they will receive adequate physical, intellectual, psychological, and spiritual care.

The future of caring is not a women's or family issue. Not only is this inaccurate, not only is it unfair. This conception of the issue simply will not lead us to any useful solutions to the problems we currently face in caring for others. Individuals and families cannot possibly promulgate the degree of revision in cultural values and practices that is needed. As Rhode (1990b) reminds us, "At stake are questions not only of gender equality, but also of cultural priorities" (211).

"The challenge," writes Friedan (1981), "is to tap our own wellspring of generative human power, accepting the political responsibility to restructure the system . . . to meet the new needs of individual growth and family" (323). Friedan is correct in stating as a culture we must restructure our collective attitude toward caring. Because the system we have historically relied on no longer functions smoothly, we are now forced to reconsider what caring is to mean and who is to do it in the United States. Perhaps, though, "forced" is not as useful a term to frame the choice before us as is "invited," since what lies before us is an unparalleled opportunity to create a better, richer way of living. Various individuals and groups have already articulated several

options. Oddly enough, these can be configured as a multiple
choice item on a test of our cultural values and our future: In
the future, care in the United States will:

> ● continue to be expected/required of women who will con-
> tinue to suffer personal and professional costs and decreas-
> ingly will be willing to do it.
> ● be provided through institutions that are paid by individu-
> als or agencies.[2]
> ● be supported and valued actively as evidenced in a wide
> range of government and institutional programs, policies,
> and incentives as well as community and individual efforts
> that make it possible to care for others without incurring
> excessive individual costs.

The only choice foreclosed to us is not choosing. Whether by
active efforts or passive deference to others who do exert their
ideas, we will create the future of caring in the United States.
To make those choices in an informed way we need to consider
both what would be required to establish caring as a cultural
priority and what the likely consequences for individuals and
the social order as a whole might be.

The Cultural Imperative: Creating a
Culture That Values Caring

Nearly a century ago, Emma Goldman (Shulman, 1972) asserted:
"Social revolution is a *fundamental transvaluation of values*. Our
institutions and conditions rest upon deep-seated ideas. To
change those conditions and at the same time leave the underlying ideas and values intact means only a superficial transformation" (354). Goldman's insight guides us yet today in realizing
that cultural practices cannot be separated from the array of
beliefs and values that undergird them. Thus, fundamental
changes in how caring is understood and practiced in the United
States cannot be effected by tinkering with a few specific programs and policies nor by advising individuals how to cope better
with the multiple, competing demands for their time and energy.
    Instead, we must from the outset understand the ongoing
dialectic between ideas and practice: what we do in our daily

lives informs what we think and believe in, just as our beliefs and values guide our concrete conduct. Mindful of this, we want to address structural issues, cultural understandings, and the interrelationships between these to define ways to remake the meaning of care. Efforts at change, then, will focus on ways to form and inform cultural priorities as well as particular social conditions, practices, and language behaviors that preclude or encourage caring for others.

Bring Care into Public Discourse

Immediately we confront a problem: caring and the concrete activities comprising it have been privatized. They transpire beneath the vision and general consciousness of the culture at large. One result of this is that we have not yet developed a public vocabulary to describe and address issues of care. The language of care seems, by conventional understandings, to be incongruous with cultural and institutional considerations (Cohen, 1991; Diamond & Hartsock, 1981; Hewlett, 1991; Petchesky, 1984). In recognizing the impoverished vocabulary we have for thinking and talking about care, Tronto (1989) comments that the need "to rethink appropriate forms of caring also raises the broadest questions about the shape of social and political institutions" (185). In effect, Tronto directs our attention to the definitional practices that comprise our culture.

One response comes from Nel Noddings (1984, 1990), who maintains the language and practice of care should remain separate from the public sphere. She situates caring exclusively in private relations, arguing that caring is a personal activity that has been and should be done for intimates. Whatever is or might be done for others beyond an individual's intimates exceeds the boundaries Noddings erects for "genuine caring."

My own position, it should be obvious, departs sharply from that of Noddings in several respects. First, she severely circumscribes the purview of caring, arguing that it occurs (that is, can and should occur) only in the most personal contexts. In limiting care to established close relationships, Noddings precludes many forms of caring, narrowing it to only what it has been historically. Further, in allowing history to demarcate the boundary of her vision, Noddings prematurely abridges the range of moral concerns that might be encompassed within a reformed understanding of what caring can and, perhaps, should be. For instance, what is to become of children, elderly, and ill people who have no families to care for them? Are we to define them as unworthy of care simply because we don't know them personally? The increased life spans and fragmented families that characterize our era make it necessary for us to ask how we provide for those who in some other time might have been cared for by families.[3]

Perhaps what is most disturbing about Noddings's position is its acceptance of the conventional bifurcation of human life into exclusive categories of public and private. In retaining caring's traditional separation from public concerns, she disallows considerations of substantive changes in social organization itself (Tronto, 1989, 181–182). Simultaneously, retaining care's placement in the private sphere sustains its invisibility and devaluation by confining it to the margins of cultural life (Cohen, 1991; Cornell, 1991). The historical location of care in the private sphere is precisely what needs to be contested now. As the long-standing separation between public and private spheres increasingly proves itself unable to meet the needs of contemporary Americans, questions, ranging from conservative to radical, are being voiced. Sapiro (1981), for instance, challenges the bifurcation by asking, "Why is an individual's relationship to the production of children not commonly accepted as a matter of political interest?" (713). In a similar vein, in their critique of interest theory as the basis of Western political systems, Diamond and Hartsock (1981) observe that "the reduction of all human emotions to interests and interests to the rational search for gain reduces the human community to an instrumental, arbitrary, and deeply unstable alliance" (719). Petchesky (1984) calls for no less than a "total revolutionary program" in which concrete social and individual needs replace abstract rights as the basis of social and political life (670).

Underlying all of these challenges is the assumption that we cannot generate effective solutions to the care problems confronting us if we circumscribe our vision by the historical and current assumptions and practices. Rather, the basic organization of cultural life must be disputed, and alternative ways of constituting the social order itself need to be imagined and analyzed (Eisenstein, 1983) to provoke fundamental transformation in our cultural attitudes toward caring (Blum, Homiak, Housman, & Scheman, 1976; Finch & Groves, 1983; Kaplan, 1982).[4]

Continuing to regard caring as a private issue partakes of precisely the assumptive frameworks that have produced the prevailing and now dysfunctional cultural configurations. Transforming what care means and who does it requires dislodging it from its historical embeddedness in only the private sphere and the realm of personal concern. Simultaneously, the association among women, caring, and the personal realm must be qualified by men's increased involvements in caregiving roles and family life. The exigence now is to situate the issue of caring squarely within public consciousness. With Tronto (1989), I believe that an effort to reform the cultural meanings "needs to begin by broadening our understanding of what caring for others means, both in terms of the moral questions it raises and in terms of the need to restructure broader social and political institutions if caring for others is to be made a more central part of the everyday lives of everyone in society" (1989, 184). Only by positioning caring within public awareness and public life will it become more integrated into the assumptions that guide the daily practices of individuals, corporations, communities, institutions, and general social intercourse. And only then will caring be salient in our cultural self-image.

The Discursive Placement of Caring in the Public Sphere

How might we go about incorporating caring into the public sphere? A first priority is to sunder caring from its conventional location in private life and name it as a cultural issue that demands ongoing and serious attention from "the public." Weedon's (1987) observation that discourse is a primary "structuring principle of society" (41) suggests a number of particular strategies and sites where we might enact them.

A first realization that Weedon provokes is that the language with which care is described will be fundamentally important in reconstructing attitudes toward it. Attention to specific language choices, for instance, is critical when instigating care talk into public discourse. Efforts to interject care talk into public locations will likely be met with tendencies (deliberate or otherwise) to construe care issues within the valuative and linguistic frameworks of the public sphere. As Diamond and Hartsock (1981), among others (Grant, 1987; Jonasdottir, 1988; Jones, 1988), point out, this could seriously distort understandings of what care is by representing it with language ill-suited to preserve its integrity. In prior chapters we have seen that acts of caring are often described as "subordination," "passivity," and "submissiveness," each of which implies a lack of agency on the part of the caregiver and each of which is at odds with the cultural ethos favoring assertiveness, ambition, and power. Care must be recast in language that dispels these associations and frees caring from its historical and discursive placement.

Naming is a powerful symbolic act for in naming something we say what it is and how it is to be regarded and valued. Just as importantly, in naming we say what something is not. A telling example of this comes from Diwakar's (1948) description of Gandhi's use of "passive resistance" as a means of promoting change. In 1906, when Gandhi led the South African Indians in a movement against unjust laws, he used the term *passive resistance* to describe what was then a new form of political protest. Later, Diwakar reports, Gandhi confessed he "felt ashamed of using an English word" that did not mean within the English language what he intended. Because English-speaking cultures revere activity, initiative, and strength, passive was disdained as the opposite of those. Later Gandhi used the term *satyagraha*, a Sanskrit word that means to hold fast to the truth. He found that his meaning for passive resistance was distorted when interpreted within the frameworks of English speakers (1).

In the sixties in this country the term *passive resistance* was again introduced, this time to describe the protest strategies of the civil rights movement. From the start, however, the Reverend Martin Luther King, Jr., systematically defined passive resistance as a movement of extraordinary power, sufficient strength, and confidence in one's own principles to suffer violence from others without responding in kind. In time, King and the strategy of passive resistance won considerable respect from the U.S. public, who came to associate it with personal, moral strength. In carefully building an association between passive resistance and strength, Reverend King was able to avoid having his meanings co-opted by the dominant social order.

The same principles apply to instigating care talk into public discourse. Renaming acts of care in language that recognizes their agency and strength will be instrumental in fashioning respect for them. What has been called "submissive," for instance, could equally well be labeled "generosity of spirit" or "non-ego-centrism"; "passivity" is also "openness to others" and sufficient strength in one's identity to yield to others; "subordination" might as accurately be described as "not needing to occupy the limelight." Consistent attention to particular language choices and the implications they have will not only be useful in shaping attitudes toward caring itself, but also in introducing into public discourse qualities and inclinations that bespeak interdependence as a kind of potency and connections with others as a reflection of personal maturity.

Clearly, then, an initial task is to be self-conscious in our efforts to develop ways of talking about caring for others that can be communicated within, but not co-opted by, the standard public forums in our society. In so doing, we begin the fundamental and powerful symbolic task of naming the issue as one appropriate for public thought and action. Then, following Goldman's lead, we recognize that the magnitude of transformation needed requires multiple strategies be employed on many fronts of cultural life.[5] For this reason, efforts to contest cultural views of women and caring must proceed simultaneously in multiple sites so that collectively they pervade cultural consciousness.

Sites for Discursive Struggle

To secure greater prominence for caring in public life, Rhode (1990a) suggests "we need greater attention to the social circumstances that would encourage such influence" (6). In elaborating this position, she advises that "to create a society truly committed to caretaking values will also require more fundamental changes . . . a broad range of initiatives" (211). The objective is to infuse talk and concerns about caring into cultural life at every turn by developing and weaving into ongoing public conversation multiple particular issues that focus attention and discussion on meeting needs for caring that currently exist as well as the perhaps greater ones that lie ahead.

Governmental Actions

To effect a transformation in cultural values and, with that, cultural practices, changes need to be introduced in multiple dimensions of public life. Governmental programs and initiatives are a logical starting point since they are both the most broad and most capable of fomenting related changes in other arenas of social life. As Moynihan (1986) incisively points out, "No government . . . can avoid having policies that profoundly influence family relationships. . . . The only question is whether these will be purposeful, intended policies or whether they will be residual, derivative, in a sense, concealed ones" (5).

In recent years the U.S. government has not done much to support family life and family needs (Chan & Momparler, 1991). Hewlett (1986) caustically notes that "children are not doing well in contemporary America, and our public policies seem to be making the situation worse, not better" (110). "It is not that we don't know how to run high-quality day-care centers," she goes on to point out. "It's just that we have decided not to allocate public resources to small children" (276). To take another example, just last year the family leave bill was resolutely vetoed by President Bush. He argued it would create hardships for business and industry, making an unequivocal statement about cultural priorities: business and industry are more important than families. The "antifamily" label for the current U.S. government is well earned and widely recognized. Government officials at all levels need to hear numerous, firm messages that their constituents regard support for families and broad human concerns as key issues that will influence voting decisions.

There are a number of very specific ways in which national, state, and local governments might elevate caring in public consciousness. For starters, consider that two of the most strongly supported proposals of the White House Council Conferences on Families were (1) developing alternative forms of good child care both inside and outside of private homes and (2) promoting policies in government, labor, and business that enable men and women to hold good jobs while participating actively in strong family life (discussed in Friedan, 1981, 108). More than a decade after these proposals were made, there's been little headway in revising laws and programs to support family life.

Another critical way in which governmental action can facilitate greater valuing of care is to provide various kinds of tax advantages and social security credit to individuals with children or others for whom they provide care. Vouchers or allowances for childcare—standard in several other countries—and for caring for elderly and disabled people might be issued, as might deductions on income taxes (Edleman, 1991; Friedan, 262; Hewlett, 1986, 1991; Sommers & Shields, 1987). The proposal for a one thousand dollar tax credit for parents made by the National Commission on Children is a start, albeit an inadequate one.

Mindful of the primary principle of capitalist systems, the government could also provide incentives in the forms of tax breaks or other advantages to profit-oriented developers and companies to build quality on-site day-care centers (Friedan, 1981, 261; Hewlett, 1986, 1991). More direct pressure to provide such programs can be applied to the multitude of agencies and institutions that receive federal funding as a condition for continued governmental support. Just as universities and social agencies are now required to meet affirmative action and EEOC laws in order to qualify for funding, they could in the future be required to expand health insurance to cover comprehensive prenatal treatment and to provide day care for children and other dependents so that employees could meet their families needs. If the officials in government are convinced that their constituents regard providing care as a critical public responsibility, they will find ways to enact changes. Through direct and indirect incentives, governments can make it advantageous for public and private enterprises to develop programs and policies that make caring for families possible without inequitable losses.

Business and Industrial Innovations

The contexts of work—labor, businesses, corporations, nonprofit agencies—also need to be apprised of their responsibilities for creating a society that encourages caring. A number of changes could heighten public consciousness of caring and alter attitudes that caring is irrelevant to worklife.[6] Some changes can be implemented relatively quickly. An urgency already well defined is providing family leaves for men and women when a child is born or adopted as well as when any family member needs special care (Friedan, 1981; Hewlett, 1986, 1991; Okin, 1989). In efforts to gain more widespread and consistent policies that address this need, it is important to articulate this consistently as a need for family leave. Arguing for maternity leaves only perpetuates traditional gender inequities that damage women, men, and children. We need language and practices that challenge what Cornell (1991) calls "the imposed convention that mothers are the primary caretakers of children" (404). As Rhode (1990b) points out, "Asymmetries in parental roles circumscribe opportunities for both sexes. . . . It is critical to develop policies that encourage paternal as well as maternal commitments . . . to recast the framework [in a way] that emphasizes not biological distinctions, but the consequences of recognizing them in particular social, political, and economic circumstances" (210).

When both parents participate in caring for children and homelife, a powerful model of gender-free caring is presented to young children. Among those who have studied children's development there is consensus that both boys and girls, as well as mothers and fathers, would be more healthy, whole, able human beings if childrearing were a parental activity, not a maternal one (Apter, 1990; Hewlett, 1986, 1991; Okin, 1989).

Yet, even *parental leaves* is not an ideal term since it restricts what counts as acceptable absence to children's needs and often to only newborn or newly adopted children's needs. When elderly or disabled family members or spouses need help, business and industry should make it possible for workers to provide it without being penalized in their jobs. The term *family leave* defines the issue as providing time for any member of a family who needs care at a given time; in so doing it locates family responsibilities within the realm of public concern.

The argument that such leaves are not financially feasible, heard often from business leaders, is simply not supported by empirical facts. The United States has the dubious distinction of having the least comprehensive and least well-supported system of child care of any developed country in the world (Hewlett, 1986, 1991). Other countries manage to stay economically productive, many of them more so than the U.S., while providing substantial leaves for new parents—usually with full pay for at least part of the time and generally for six to twelve months (Beck et al., 1990; Hewlett, 1986). The United States can do better by its children and families, and labor and business need to lead the way. To bring about adequate childcare, we should simultaneously urge government to provide incentives and businesses to respond to legitimate employee needs.

Along with family leaves, flexible schedules and the option of part-time status as students and/or workers are priorities for parents (Hewlett, 1991; Noddings, 1990, 172). There is simply no reason that many business, labor organizations, and educational systems cannot offer workers schedules that allow them to take care of family responsibilities as well as to work full days if they choose or part time if that allows them to meet better their families' needs. As Janeway (1971) pointed out fully two decades ago, "Steady part-time workers can solve some of their [industry's] problems and are worth training . . . a young woman with a child might take her law degree part time over five years just as well as full time over three" (190). The rigid, uniform expectations that were perhaps functional fifty years ago are ill-suited to the nature and needs of contemporary Americans. Further, if we as a society wish to say that caring for others is "a valued social activity, then there should be no sacrifice in either work or pay" (Cornell, 1991, 404).

Another much needed change in the world of work is adaptable benefits plans (Friedan, 1981; Noddings, 1990). The old, one-size-fits-all design doesn't actually fit the needs of the majority of today's workers. In a society where only 7 percent of families fit the traditional nuclear family model, old plans designed for that conventional structure are unsuitable. At little or no cost business and industry could allow individual workers to select benefits that best meet their diverse needs (Friedan, 271). Given such choice, a single mother might forego vacation for additional medical coverage for her children, while a childfree couple might opt for more vacation days and fewer family leave days, a gay couple might prefer increased retirement benefits to extensive life insurance, and so forth. Allowing individuals to tailor benefits within the constraints of standard established limits on total benefits would enable workers to care responsibly. Individuals can exercise influence by proposing changes in benefit programs in their places of employment and by including questions about benefits in their job interviewing. Naming these as issues in work-life furthers the integration of care into public life.

Business, industry, and education also need to redesign schedules for advancement in ways that acknowledge without penalty the responsibilities of caring entailed in having families. Universities, for instance, might lengthen the time before which a new faculty member is evaluated for permanent tenure if she or he has one or more children or any family member with special needs during the initial appointment. Parallel adjustments need to be made in firms' formal or informal timetables dictating when to evaluate an associate's qualifications for promotion to partner as well as in any businesses where there are understood times at which workers are expected to advance to a next level.

The kinds of changes needed from business and industry are not likely to be conceived, much less implemented, by executives and managers who are unaware of and/or insensitive to ways in which employees' needs have changed in the past couple of decades, nor will such thinking be common to all supervisors. Thus, managers and executives need to be trained in a whole range of human skills (Friedan, 1981, 271) that enable them to recognize workers as whole people leading whole lives that include, yet go beyond their jobs. Various training and development programs will be needed to inform supervisory personnel of issues that they are expected to devote time and effort to managing.

Changes in Educational Institutions

Because schools are primary contexts of socialization, there are important ways in which they can be instrumental in redefining America's understanding of what caring for others is to mean. At a minimum, schools of all levels should adopt the changes identified for professions in general. This is important not just because it responds to faculty's responsibilities for caring, but also because it models that ethic for students: when they see faculty and staff take time off for family needs they will learn to accept this as normal and appropriate in any worker's life.

Beyond this, schools can institute a number of curricular changes that carry the implicit message that caring is everyone's business, not just women's (Noddings, 1990). All students should, of course, be exposed to literature and textbooks that represent the importance of caring for all humans, but this alone is not enough. Okin (1989) recommends curricular revisions that dissuade students from thinking anyone's life and activities are constrained by sex. Boys and girls might be enrolled in home economics courses as well as family life classes.

Additionally, all students should be taught in history and social studies programs, among other sites, about gender inequities in marriage and social expectations and their consequences as well as about discrimination in the workplace. Incorporating discussions of care concerns into classes on government and civics is also important in the multifaceted effort to define caring as a public issue. By infusing curricula with this kind of consciousness we cultivate an awareness of and respect for caring in those who will be the future parents as well as leaders in business, industry, government, and education.

Schools can also develop programs to retrain individuals whose jobs disappear. Friedan points out that the sizable number of laid-off workers from factories and dying industries could be prepared for caregiving careers where there is a severe shortage of skilled workers. Nursing, day care, and social work are but a few of the areas in which we need more qualified people. Good retraining programs would be a boon for society and individuals whose old jobs have disappeared.

Schools can also do much to influence what is defined as professional by making strategic choices about how to describe and discuss particular kinds of jobs and careers. For instance, Noddings (1990) points out that the quest to be "true professionals" is in direct conflict with valuing personal contact that requires what is referred to as "menial labor" (169). The language we use to describe professionalism divorces it from direct human contact, which may, as Noddings suggests, demand that we engage in "a careful redefinition of what it means to be a professional" (169). It goes without saying that such redefinition must entail making direct contact and care jobs attractive by imbuing them with symbolic status and material rewards (Friedan, 1981, 267).

Individual and Community Efforts

Let us not neglect significant ways in which individuals and communities can contribute to making caring more salient in the life of our culture. Individuals acting independently and in concert can be instrumental in altering a culture's understanding of its concerns. One of the most significant yet frequently overlooked means of legitimating new topics on a culture's agenda is communication, both informal and formal. It is a political act to introduce care talk into conversations with colleagues, acquaintances, social and civic associates, and friends. Ordinary talk about personal experiences in caring for others and, more broadly, about needs for care as a cultural priority comprises an argument that these topics are ones of public interest.

Individuals can also be more overtly political through petitions that demand communities include care-related issues in the agenda for meetings of county commissioners, town councils, and other civic and governmental bodies at local levels. At first, requests for attention to issues like creating a community day-care center or an elder social club may be greeted with surprise or discomfort from officials not accustomed to considering such topics "public business"; as the requests continue and the topics are discussed, however, perceptions will shift in recognition of what has been now defined as a public concern.

More organized, structural changes can also be implemented at the community level, in some cases as a result of decisions made at local meetings. Friedan (1981) discusses at length quality day-care centers that are conceived and run by neighborhoods. Typically these are run as cooperatives in which each family in a neighborhood contributes to the responsibilities of operating a center. More of these could be designed to provide good and ideally accessible care for children. A desirable side effect of localized centers is their potential to enhance a sense of community and interdependence.

In tandem and in addition, communities as well as whole towns and states might think innovatively about different ways to use public spaces (Friedan, 261). In many areas there are buildings that once housed various governmental offices but now are vacant. Other public spaces such as churches and schools are not occupied part of the time. There are a number of ways such spaces might be used, often with no or few renovations, to provide care to various people. For instance, a social club for elderly, ideally with transportation provided, would respond to the loneliness and isolation many older people experience as lifetime companions disappear through deaths and relocations.

Some communities report great success with centers that simultaneously meet the care needs of children, who need supervision and interaction, and older citizens, who are lonely, have free time, and often welcome purposeful activities. Dubbed "granny nannies," many of these elderly people enjoy their roles in childrens' lives just as many children appreciate time with older people (Brody, 1989–1990). Vacant or underused spaces might also be designated as day-care facilities as might churches when congregational needs allow. Grassroots initiatives in communities provide ways for individuals to create contexts and social arrangements that respond to needs for caring, all the while repeating the larger message that caring is a public issue.

Parenting Practices

Let us not overlook the private enclave of the home, which is a primary arena for inculcating awareness of caring as a cultural priority. Noted authority on child development Marion Wright Edleman (1991), when asked where we begin to transform the United States into a society supportive of caring and of children, gave this response: "Within ourselves in our own homes and schools and neighborhoods" (77). Edleman highlights the critical influence of parents whose conduct and beliefs teach children how to see themselves and others and what kinds of activities, attitudes, and values are appropriate for various people. When young children see both parents engage in cooking, cleaning, and childcare, they are likely to develop expectations of themselves and others not restricted by traditional sex roles. When daddy, as well as mommy, takes time from work to nurse a sick child or other relative, children learn caring is appropriate for men as well as women. And when mothers, as well as fathers, sometimes delegate or defer a child's request in order to pursue an individual interest, children learn that women, as well as men, have lives and interests apart from others. Children who overhear parents discussing how various candidates for offices stand on care issues will deduce that these are concerns of public life.

The language we use to describe care activities and those who engage in them is as important in the family context as elsewhere. For instance, the common reference to a husband's "helping" his wife with cooking or cleaning implies that these are really *her* jobs and, further, that the husband is doing something extraordinary and worthy of gratitude when he involves himself in homelife. Chodorow (1978) points out a similar linguistic slip concerning men's roles as fathers when she notes that "men 'babysit' their own children; women do not" (179). Our language currently offers no male parallel to women's "mothering." Sometimes we speak of "parenting" and even less often of "fathering," but most often men who engage intensely in caring for children are said to be "mothering." Surely, we can find a way to talk and think about distinctively male caring.

The plethora of concrete activities and discursive practices comprising family life profoundly influences a child's understandings of what it means to be a man or a woman and, consequently, how they will constitute their own masculinity or femininity. This is precisely Chodorow's point in focusing on parenting patterns as not only the basis of identity development, but also a primary means of changing how we, as men and women, see ourselves and each other. Designating the family as a primary context for changing attitudes toward caring and women, Chodorow argues that "equal parenting would leave people of both genders with the positive capacities each has, but without the destructive extremes these currently tend toward" (1978, 218). Her landmark book concludes with this statement: "The elimination of the present organization of parenting in favor of a system of parenting in which both men and women are responsible would be a tremendous social advance. . . . Such advances . . . depend on the conscious organization and activity of all women and men who recognize that their interests lie in transforming the social organization of gender and eliminating sexual inequality" (219).

Synergetic Change

The array of changes identified here need not overwhelm us, particularly if we believe the goals worthy of sizable effort. Each of us need only contribute in particular ways in specific contexts and at selective times. In concert, our individual actions can work synergetically so that over time they restructure how our society evaluates and teaches its members to think about caring, men and women, and the essence of public life.

Clearly my parsing of changes into discrete levels from government to community is more a matter of analytic convenience than a description of "reality." The particular initiatives I've pointed out are not isolated from one another but interact in ways that potentially multiply the impact of each one. Whatever programs and policies the government implements, for instance, reverberate throughout cultural life, providing an impetus for changes in business, industry, schools, and communities. Likewise curricular modifications to emphasize caring as part of social life will be felt in communities, businesses, labor, and, eventually, government as children and students grow up and take the priorities and values they have learned into their various civic, professional, and personal circumstances. An inventive idea that works in one community may function as a model for other communities until, grassroots fashion, what was originally an innovation may become standard practice throughout the United States.

There are a number of interrelated ways a culture constitutes its values and names its priorities. Laws and governmental policies announce a society's principles and goals, sometimes leading attitude and opinion (Cohen, 1991; Cornell, 1991). Policies and normative understandings in corporations, labor, and civic affairs reflect and, in turn, promote expectations of conduct. Salaries, prestige, and language associated with various jobs connote their importance in a culture. And we should not underrate the importance of everyday conversations in which caring is described in ways that demonstrate esteem and that position it at the hub of cultural life. So, in a number of material and symbolic ways a culture engages in the ongoing process of defining its beliefs and, in so doing, establishing guidelines for individual and collective practice.

Currently our laws, governmental and business policies, educational institutions, and communities coalesce to define caring as outside of the purview of public life and public concern. That can be changed, however, through particular activities that usher in a diversity of initiatives and redefinitions in a gradual, systematic manner. Engaging in enough of these activities over time has the potential to promulgate a veritable transformation in our culture's attitude toward caring, what it means, and whose concern it is. Envisioning that possible future is the focus of the final section in this chapter.

Life in a Culture That Values Caring

Growing out of its historical location in the lives of women and others who have been designated in some sense inferior by the culture, caring is now generally regarded as outside of the concerns of public life and of men. Yet, care's association with women and private life results from certain historical, social, and political practices, which means it can be contested and changed. We have noted an array of circumstances, programs, policies, and individual actions that would cultivate new attitudes toward caring, those who do it, and its place in cultural life. It now remains for us to imagine, as Janeway (1971) puts it, what it would be like to live in this transformed social world that we could agree to believe in.

In imagining this reformed world we begin by dissociating caring from circumstances of subordination that may have historically surrounded them. Janeway, for instance, notes as virtues for all people "patience and endurance . . . awareness of emotional atmosphere and personal relationships" (111). Janeway then goes on to argue that "a larger awareness of the human context would profit us all in a world where the human context grows more important every day, where individual action becomes harder and harder, and where we desperately need to agree on how to work together toward common ends" (112). The kinds of insights and orientations cultivated by caring for others, in short, can enrich individuals and the overall culture.

Chodorow (1990) concurs, noting that a "relational self," one that is involved with and cares for others, "enables empathy, nurturance and intimacy" (121).[7] Earlier chapters have revealed that being taught to think of oneself as interdependent with others and to recognize and respond to their needs are cornerstones in developing an inclination to care for others. Appreciating the profound interconnections among humans enables all individuals, regardless of age, sex, race, or class, to understand

and participate in life in ways forever closed to those whose rigid autonomy diminishes their capacity to form intimate relationships and to appreciate differences. There are many consequences of this deprivation that merit greater recognition than they have so far received in our culture. One repercussion is dishonest or restricted relationships, which diminish possibilities for understanding oneself and others. Based on her observations, Miller (1986) concludes that rigidly autonomous individuals "are denied an essential part of life— the opportunity to acquire self-understanding through knowing their impact on others. They are thus deprived of 'consensual validation,' feedback . . . valid knowledge about [others]" (10). When the depth of involvements is limited, insights into self and others are narrowed corollatively; in not having such insights a whole dimension of human experience is lost.

Individuals who allow themselves to empathize with others, to understand the world as they see and feel it, and to care about responding to their needs for comfort and contact enlarge their own understanding of the human condition and themselves. That women have historically been more advanced in emotional awareness than men results, at least in large part, from socialization that emphasizes caregiving by females. Miller points out that "we have created a situation in which men's allowing themselves in a primary way to be attuned to the needs of others and to serve others threatens them" (71). Because "manhood" has been defined by self-interest, competitiveness, individualism, and rigid autonomy, men have been discouraged from the particular and valuable kinds of knowledge, satisfaction, and growth available only through intense involvement in human relationships. By deemphasizing genderized divisions of labor and concern, we open the realm of emotional life and learning to men in ways that enlarge them (Cornell, 1991; Halpern, 1987).

Further, we should note that the qualities historically esteemed in our culture and held out as ideals for men may no longer be the most functional for the challenges and needs of today and the future. "We have," warns Miller, "reached the end of the road that is built on the set of traits held out for male identity— advance at any cost, pay any price, drive out all competitors, and kill them if necessary. . . . It now seems clear we have arrived at a point from which we must seek a basis of faith in connection—

and not only faith but recognition that it is a requirement for the existence of human beings. [This is] the basis for what seem the absolutely essential next steps in Western history if we are to survive" (88).

For years a rising chorus in the Western world has bemoaned the breakdown of communities and families, has foreseen that interaction with technology may be substituted for involvement in human relationships, has offered eulogies for our impoverished understandings of ourselves and natural rhythms of life. As laments only, these are as pointless as they are poignant since mourning bygone values leads us nowhere. Instead, we might better channel our collective discomfort into emerging efforts to challenge the inevitability of this prophesy of gloom and doom.

Punctuating contemporary society is the active searching for alternatives to our current ways of living and working. Some U.S. businesses have realized that teamwork is sometimes more productive and satisfying than individual assignments, cooperation may be more effective than competition as a means to heighten motivation and achievement, attending to human needs may enhance accomplishments rather than detract from them. Impressed by mounting evidence from researchers, success stories in other countries where worklife accommodates human needs, and halting experiments in our own land, some U.S. businesses have begun to move toward a new model—one that is more flexible and responsive to individuals' needs. And many of the businesses trying this new model report it is better suited to contemporary conditions than traditional emphases on power over others, competitive individualism, and unyielding standards and policies applied to all, regardless of individual circumstances and needs.

Insights into the kinds of values missing and needed in Western culture are perhaps not new. What is new, however, is the perspective from which we can now consider what kind of people we want to be and what will be required to realize this vision. Liberated from its historical situatedness in the private sphere and women's domain, we can now recover the idea of caring as a responsibility and privilege of us all and as a central concern of public life. To do this is the necessary first step in recreating our culture so that it esteems care as central to public life and invites us all to engage in it.

With this, we open the possibility of constructing a society in which all members are expected to care for others and in which all members are given access to the particular kinds of learnings and qualities that are cultivated through awareness of interdependence and involvement in relationships with others. In such a culture all members could participate in processes that sustain life. A culture centrally concerned with caring for others is an august vision, one that holds out the prospect that we might all become more life affirming, life enhancing, and life revering.

The analysis made in this chapter focuses our attention on questioning the existing organization of our culture by challenging its long-standing associations of caring with women and the private sphere. Breaking these associations through a variety of discursive strategies is a critical initial step in reforming our understandings of care and, ultimately, of ourselves and the kind of individuals and society we might imagine ourselves to be. It is fully possible—if we but invest the imagination and effort—to create a world that is better than the present one, to create a society that can proudly judge itself by the principle Moynihan (1986) articulates: "The qualities of a civilization may be measured by how it cares for its elderly. Just as surely, the future of a society may be measured by how it cares for its young" (194).

I am well aware that reports of sex differences can be used to rationalize oppression, and I deplore any use of my work for this purpose. But I do not see it as empowering to encourage women to put aside their own concerns and perceptions.

—Carol Gilligan, *Reply*

CHAPTER 8
Conclusion

"No," we might respond to Gilligan, "it is not empowering to tell women to put aside their own concerns and perceptions. Neither, however, is it empowering to tell them to disregard the contexts in which they exercise those concerns and perceptions and from which consequences will be imposed on them."

My aim in this book has been to fill in the context that Gilligan neglected by situating caring for others within the historical and contemporary circumstances of its occurrence. This, I hope, enables us to better understand what care has come to mean in our society, the structural and symbolic forces that sustain those meanings, and sites and strategies whereby we may contest established views of caring and women.

Clearly Gilligan intended for her description of women's different voice to affirm and empower women, but as Weedon (1987) cautions, we cannot regard "authorship as a guarantee of meaning" (163). What Gilligan did or did not intend, while perhaps of interest, is beside the point in assessing how her work has been interpreted and the ramifications it can have for individuals who enact her view of women. Because any text is polysemous, it permits multiple interpretations. One reading of *In a Different Voice* is a distinctly conservative one that affirms traditional sex roles and accepts their equally traditional consequences. Encrusted sex roles have for centuries relegated both women and caring to the periphery of Western culture and denied men access to important dimensions of human life and personal development (Rosenblum, 1989).

I encountered this conservative response to Gilligan's work in conversations with colleagues, friends, relatives, and students, and I became concerned about the consequences of embracing and enacting care as she presented it. Many women with whom I talked saw Gilligan as legitimating their tendencies to care for others, regardless of the inequities of assigning that task only to certain groups and the personal and social costs of assuming the role of caretaker in our society. On the other hand, men often seemed to find in Gilligan's work a justification for continuing to rely on women and to excuse themselves from the responsibilities of caring for others.

During the time when I was first hearing these interpretations of Gilligan's ideas, I was deeply involved in caring for my terminally ill mother. This experience of direct and sustained caregiving allowed me to understand in enlarged ways both costs and rewards of ongoing commitment to another person. The time with mother and my increasing professional interest in this topic enhanced my belief that caring for others is essential and should be a widely embraced priority. Simultaneously, these concurrent experiences heightened my awareness that, no matter how important, it can be extremely costly, even self-negating, if only some people are expected to care for others and if they do so in the context of a culture that does not value caring.

These, then, became three threads I wove throughout this inquiry: caring for others is both essential and potentially enlarging. For caring to be safe for caregivers, it must be broadly supported and enacted, rather than relegated to particular groups of people. Our culture itself must be reformed in ways that dissociate caring from its historical affiliations with women and private relationships and redefine it as a centrally important and integral part of our collective public life.

In closing this book, I want to reflect on the issues and arguments comprising my inquiry into women, care, and culture. I hope the analysis offered here will contribute to recognition of the need to transform our understandings of caring through its efforts to elucidate the historical situations and discursive practices that have constructed caring's marginal position within our culture and to point to alternative discursive activities that could contest existing meanings of care and legitimize a much different one.

I have argued that cultural conceptions of caring are impoverished by the ways in which caring has been situated historically
and by discursive practices that sustain that location. Particularly
obscured are understandings of the strengths and values of caring for others. Primary in changing this, I maintain, is reframing
the meaning of care by challenging conventional interpretations
of caring as weak, passive, and subordinate and by contesting
associations among care, women, and the private sphere. Consistent efforts to implicate care concerns in the domain of public
discourse and to accentuate its values comprise means to reform
the meaning of care in Western culture. With that might emerge
a reformed understanding of culture itself—of who we, as a
people, are and will be.

A full account of caring must situate the concrete activities
that constitute care and the constructed attitudes about them
within cultural, political, and personal horizons of meanings. In
my inquiry I have shown that our culture is facing a crisis born
of the mounting needs for care and steadily decreasing abilities
to provide it within current practices and assumptions. While we
had only three million people over the age of sixty-five at the
turn of the century, we now have over twenty-five million; by
the time we enter the next century, that number is expected to
exceed thirty-two million (Halpern, 1987). Many of our elderly
citizens require care, constant or occasional, and we have not
created the resources, policies, and practices to provide it. Children continue to be born and, just as surely, continue to need
care, especially during their early years. As the number of people
needing care rises, the number willing and able to provide it is
diminishing. It is this confluence of forces that constitutes the
care crisis we confront. And it is within these circumstances that
I situate my inquiry into who cares.

Historically, "women" has been the answer to the question of
who cares. Yet this answer is no longer viable. As a group,
women are no longer willing to have their roles assigned, their
identities conferred, and their value judged by what they do for
others. With all citizens, women demand the inalienable right to
"the pursuit of happiness," which for many includes working as
a primary focus. Other women pursue happiness by centering
their lives on caring for others, yet resist and resent the devaluation and social disenfranchisement that historically have accom-

panied this choice. And many women, perhaps the majority, believe the two choices should not be mutually exclusive: it should be possible to live and to work, to have a family and a job, and to do both with competence, dignity, and, perhaps, even joy.

My analysis demonstrates that material, structural obstacles imposed by current social institutions and practices mitigate against caring as an important, but not exclusive focus of life. The existing expectations and structures of our society make it extraordinarily difficult for one to be both a good caretaker and a good worker. Without support ranging from family leaves and tax credits to flextime and day care for elders and children, workers are crippled in their efforts to meet responsibilities to families. We need to reconfigure political and business practices in ways that enable employees to do their jobs without neglecting their families and to care for their families without jeopardizing the security or quality of their work.

The structural barriers that impede caring arise out of discourses that construct and sustain our understandings of who we are, what a "responsible worker" is, and where concerns about caring for others can and cannot be appropriately voiced. For this reason, any changes in institutional practices must be predicated upon numerous and broad discursive interventions that redefine understandings of care, women, and culture.

Through a variety of specific discursive efforts, some of which I have articulated, we can contest the encrusted bifurcation of private and public worlds, reconstruct caring in terms of its strengths and its legitimate situation in the public, as well as private, life, and redefine both women and men in ways that invite each to participate in caring for others without designating either sex as the primary caregiver. Thus, just as institutions and practices organize social life, so is each of these structured by discourse that establishes and sustains the meanings of our conduct and our lives. Through our concrete, daily activities we embody or challenge existing understandings of how and by whom things are done and what has value in our culture.

By extension, effective strategies to reform the meaning of care must be similarly situated within cultural practice. I argue that to gain a hearing, efforts to redefine what care is and to whom it is of concern need to enter into the existing discursive formations and patterns of public life by recognizing and adapting to, without being co-opted by, ready-made discursive frameworks. In pointing to discourse as a primary means for instigating symbolic and structural change, I depart from the position adopted by many others, especially Carol Gilligan.

Like Noddings, Gilligan holds that caring is valuable because it is intrinsically good. From there she argues that women should recognize their inclinations to care for others as virtues and should affirm these by and for themselves, despite their membership in a culture that does not generally value caring or those who do it. She acknowledges, but explicitly dismisses as unimportant, the consequences of engaging in activities devalued by the surrounding social order: "That women's embeddedness in lives of relationship, their orientation to interdependence, their subordination of achievement to care, and their conflicts over competitive success leave them personally at risk in mid-life seems more a commentary on the society than a problem in women" (171). Of course, the costs of caring to women represent a commentary on the society, yet that is a wholly unsatisfying stance and surely no basis for encouraging women to continue enduring those costs.

Gilligan's view of caring and her advocacy of this as a focus in women's lives strip caring out of its placement in political, economic, and social milieu, which have defined it as a low cultural priority and those who engage in it as subordinate (Janeway, 1971; Miller, 1986; Puka, 1990; Scott, 1986). Without understanding the complex contexts in which both women and caring have been located, we risk oversimplification of the issues involved. Kerber (1986), and before her, Dubois (1979), warned that reifying and rigidly dichotomizing the public and private spheres of life can lead to a focus on "women's culture" that is uninformed by larger understandings of historical processes of which it is a part and which are implicated in the meanings it has come to have. Such a decontextualized focus on women's lives and voices invites well-intentioned, but seriously misguided affirmations of what have been women's traditional activities. Further, notes Kerber (1986), this ahistorical view cannot address "the ways that [women's traditional activities] have restrained and confined women" (308; also see Cohen, 1991; Cornell, 1991).

In encouraging women to continue caring for others because it is good, it needs to be done, and no one else will do it, Gilligan invites women to participate—or to continue participating—in their own subordination. In effect, Gilligan's ideas in no way challenge the structure of our culture, which establishes the meanings and consequences of the role she advocates for women.[1] Given this, Gilligan emerges as a distinctly conservative voice, one that endorses the existing social organization and women's conventional place within it. She suggests, in fact, that *because* caring and relationships are not esteemed in Western culture, women have a special mission to be the ones who preserve these values within the pockets and margins of a social order they are not invited to collaborate in creating.

In opening her book, Gilligan (1982) notes that "woman's place in man's life cycle has been that of nurturer, caretaker, and helpmate, the weaver of those networks of relationships" (17). As a historical observation Gilligan's point is perhaps more true than not. Gilligan goes on, however, to state "woman's place in man's life cycle is to protect this recognition . . . of the continuing importance of attachment in the human life cycle" (23). Here Gilligan accepts historical contingency as inevitability and side-steps the question of whether this is how women and men *should* continue to define themselves and each other. In positioning women within man's life cycle, Gilligan subordinates women and their concerns to those of a larger arena which men define and direct. Rather than arguing for a society conjointly defined by all its members, one that incorporates values and activities histori-cally representative of different sexes, races, and classes, Gilligan seems content to leave women and caring on the fringes of "man's world."

By consenting to the existing social structure and the tenuous places women and care occupy within it, Gilligan foresakes the opportunity to identify possibilities for alternative organizations that might be more inclusive of diverse interests, concerns, and values and that might alleviate the penalties that typically accom-pany caretaking. She elects to be an observer of the social world, rather than a critic. In so defining her role, she is unable to exercise the critical instinct that "insists that what is can be disas-sembled and improved . . . goes against the grain of a legitimation process endemic to power formulations [and] the inscription on the face of social practices which says 'Do not tamper with me for I am good, just, and eternal'" (Poster, 1989, 3). For her part, Gilligan appears to accept encrusted inscriptions and not to tamper with social practices.

For my part, I have chosen to act more as a critic, first to reveal how existing structures define and constrain our ability to care for others and how those structures are sustained through discourse. I have also advocated resisting the necessity of existing structures, pointing to ways they might be disassembled and reorganized to allow fuller lives for all who participate in the culture. Involvement in caring for others offers everyone insights into self, others, human relationships, and the overall web of life. After all, as Kirkegaard (1957) reminds us, it is impossible to understand life without understanding death, impossible to understand light without understanding darkness, impossible to understand joy without understanding sickness and dread. Engaging in caring facilitates these understandings, which should be accessible to all of us—women and men alike, a point with which Gilligan clearly agrees.

Accomplishing this, however, is contingent upon contextualizing care and women within historical and current patterns of value and meaning so that we may identify practices and structures that sustain social arrangements. Following that, what is required is concerted, prolonged, and pluralistic efforts to enter into multiple discursive sites in ways capable of fomenting radical reform of cultural structure and practices. Through a range of discursive strategies it is possible to constitute a social organization that values caring and regards it as a public concern and a responsibility of all citizens.

I have picked up where Gilligan left off by enlarging the account of caring she offered. Whereas Gilligan confined her observations and advocacy to the lives and moral choices of individual women, I have centered my analysis on the structure and praxis of the culture itself. Only by changing those, I believe, can we position caring centrally in the life of our culture and all of its members; and only if this happens, can we as a people look ahead to a future that is more humane, more humanly rich than the one we have thus far created.

If the inquiry that I have been engaged in here has been at all successful, then it will be in its efforts to challenge the long-standing associations of caring with women and the private sphere. In turn, dissociating these may liberate our understandings of care and—ultimately—of ourselves and the kind of society we might imagine and agree with each other to live in.

For caring to be "safe" for women—or anyone—it must be practiced in contexts that neither assume nor create subjugation of those who engage in it. This can happen, as I have tried to show, only if caring is defined as a priority of the culture. But, returning to Gilligan's position, to argue that women should affirm and act on their learned tendencies to care regardless of how caring and caregivers are regarded is politically naive and potentially regressive for women. Such advocacy is unmindful of historical contexts, including especially entrenched associations of caring with the private sphere and subordinate status.

My mother lived in accord with Gilligan's view of woman's identity, and she suffered the predictable consequences of diminished autonomy, self-esteem, and status. I wish mother's commitment to caring for others had been more valued by the culture and less costly for her personally. Many women and men of my own generation have resisted and challenged the cultural views that so constrained our mothers' options. Yet our work is not finished. Confronting us now is the unprecedented responsibility and opportunity to effect substantial changes in how our culture defines and values caring so that women, along with men, may care for others without endangering themselves.

I hope, as my mother did, that our sons and daughters will live out richer, fuller views of women, men, and caring than have heretofore been possible in America.

Notes

References

Name Index

Subject Index

Notes

2. Who Cares in Contemporary
Western Culture?

1. The bifurcation of the world into public and private spheres is among the most thoroughly encrusted assumptions of our culture. The private sphere, which is the traditional site where caring and concerns about it are appropriate, has of course been regarded as "woman's domain." Critiques of this can be found in writings from more than a century ago. Gilman, for instance, writing in 1899, recognized domestic relations as both the primary cause of women's social oppression and the major focus of their lives. See Engles (1884/1967) and Gilman (1899/1966).
2. In later chapters I discuss in some detail the paradox built into this statement. To affirm simultaneously individualism and traditional sex roles is not possible, since the traditional sex role assigned to women has been decidedly not individualistic, but relational. See, for instance, Cohen (1991) and Cornell (1991).

3. Women, Caring, and the
Burden of Selflessness

1. I do not mean to imply here an essentialist conception of caring, nor one especially of women. My point is that women, as they are defined within the culture, are assigned the role of caring, as it is defined within the culture. Obviously each woman enacts caring in a particular way reflecting her own motives, style, abilities, and understanding of the requirements of the role. It follows from this that each incidence of caring will have its own particularities and will not be identical to any other. The diversity in women and caring notwithstanding, it is important to understand the ways in which discursive practices in the culture create reified, essentialized definitions of both women and caring, and that is the point of my analysis and the meaning of my use of the singular terms—women and caring—for what are incontestably diverse phenomena.
2. Whether this stance is "truly" universal is open to question. It can be argued that rather than applying a universal perspective which incorporates all perspectives, the standpoint advocated by Kohlberg and others including Hobbes, Hume, and Kant is actually better

conceived as substitutionalist. This line of reasoning holds that what is called universal by moral theorists is really a perspective based on a particular group, invariably a privileged group such as white, Anglo-Saxon, heterosexual, middle- to upper-class, Protestant males. To act as if this group is representative of all humans is to silence the voices and the needs of all less-privileged members of a culture. Thus, some feminist critics of science insist the allegedly universal perspective is necessarily partial, local, historical, and subjective in its positioning. See Bordo (1987) and Harding (1991).

3. The rigid dichotomy between reason and feeling has been the subject of much recent critique. Particularly penetrating analyses are offered by Bleier (1986), Harding (1987, 1991), and Keller (1985).

4. It is, of course, possible for a caregiver to confuse her or his needs with those of the cared for. This may happen when a caregiver has inadequate understandings of her/his own needs and motives and/ or when s/he has unresolved issues which may then be worked out through projections onto the cared for. This may occur easily with children (see Chodorow, 1978; Miller, 1981) or with parents with whom one has a history, complete with resentments, angers, and longings. See Keniston (1965) and Tronto (1989).

4. Gilligan's Rhetorical Construction of "Woman"

1. In using the terms *scholar* and *partisan*, I do not mean to imply these are mutually exclusive roles, and certainly not that they are oppositional ones. It is abundantly clear that all scholarship is imbued with values and, therefore, inherently partisan. In this essay I distinguish between the scholar and the partisan by conventions, understandings, and goals characteristic of each. This would imply, for instance, that scholars' advocacy grows out of and explicates evidence, reasoning, and careful inspection of materials; and her or his partisan claims do not exceed what these resources support. The pure partisan, by contrast, advances claims not demonstrably grounded in any convincing material such as data, experience, or argument and urges belief and action that is not supported by such resources. While I am clearly not suggesting these voices cannot operate in harmony, I am arguing that they do not achieve this in Gilligan's book.

2. A distinction should be recognized between connectedness as defining self by an external source and connectedness as a context within which to discover and develop self. To learn about oneself from the process of relationships is not the same as learning who one is from

others' reflections. I am indebted to Erica Rothman, M.S.W., for clarifying this distinction.

3. Articulating this rationale, Hartsock (1983) defined woman not by essential traits but rather by the "material circumstances of women's lives [that] predispose them to experience self in relation to others, to reject dualisms, to value the concrete, and to feel connected with others and nature" (242). She then argues that feminist-standpoint theory should focus on political struggle that creates "areas of social life modeled on" these traits (261).

4. Discussion of problems inherent in essentialist views of women has emerged widely. Ferguson (1988) argues that "the very insistence on the category of 'woman' has a totalizing impact that tends to blur articulation of diversities among women and men" (73) and "disabling in its lack of distinctions" (74). It is also argued that essentialist views err in presuming that all women are alike, or alike in essential respects, regardless of their diverse experiences, classes, ethnic identifications, and races. Feminism for too long has been the story and goals of white, middle-class, heterosexual women; the images of woman's nature, needs, and goals were hers, and, by implication, excluded those of all other women (Hull, Scott, & Smith, 1982; Meese, 1986; Stack, 1986).

5. It could be argued that demonstrations of care and understanding are self-defining rather than a fulfillment of expectations imposed by society and particular, proximate others. Such an argument, however, assumes that one's ability to define self operates at least largely independent of the values, history, and hegemony of the culture within which it exists. I am not unsympathetic with the position articulated by Gilligan and others that devaluing care and other activities traditionally enacted by women reflects distorted, destructive values in society itself, and that it is society and not the ethic of caring that needs to be reformed. That notwithstanding, until and unless those caring are accorded widespread respect within the culture, those who engage in it will retain marginal, subordinate status and the discriminations incumbent in such status.

5. The Genesis of Women's Tendency to Care

1. This is not to suggest that there are only three explanations. There are numerous ways in which explanations can be divided and grouped. One explanation that I have chosen not to deal with maintains that there is a biological basis for feminine behaviors. Clearly there are biological differences between women and men, yet the

consensus of opinion among researchers is increasingly that biology determines little, if anything, about human behavior since it too is subject to editing by social and cultural influences. Biology may establish a certain relatively immutable limits on behaviors and capacities, but these seem meager. Thus, my focus is on the influences that shape "sexed beings" into socially and culturally gendered ones. For further discussion, see Chodorow (1978, esp. 13–29).

2. I place quotes around Gilligan's "ethic of care" to indicate that she has not yet made a convincing demonstration that the tendencies to care she observed comprise an ethic. A careful reading of her book, which reports the major data and interpretations on which her claim rests, reveals that the levels in moral development she theorizes are not necessarily sequential in occurrence. Further, her interviews indicate that people move "back" as well as "forward" in what she terms a "progression toward an ethic of moral maturity." Finally, not a single one of the cases she presents entail a person's moving through all three of the levels she posits, making it difficult to conclude that what she has identified is indeed a progression toward an ethic. For further discussion, see Broughton (1983) and Puka (1990).

3. Chodorow's account is not to be confused with the social-psychological process of internalizing roles. She quite clearly distinguishes her analysis of the process of self-formation from that offered by social psychology. The latter emphasizes internalizing into self roles that were once external, which necessarily assumes some preexisting, albeit rudimentary, self into which socially defined roles can be placed. By contrast, Chodorow argues that it is psychological processes, specifically introjection and identification, through which a basic self is actually formed. Her account insists that the core self-characteristic of females—the essence of an individual's personality—results from the child's introjection and identification with the mother such that the mother's identity is formative of the child's; it is not merely added to that of the child. The centrality of these very early processes to personality development explains why Chodorow's account of female development places emphasis atypical of psychoanalytic formulations on the special significance of the preoedipal phase in psychic development. Female infants early introjection of and identification with mothers is compounded during the oedipal phase, during which the girls (unlike the boys) do not have to give up their attachments to mothers. Consequently, argues Chodorow, females retain both mothers and fathers as attachment figures, yielding a substantially more complex and rich inner object-world than boys can generate since they have separated from their mothers.

4. Chodorow (1978) quite clearly recognizes the pervasive and powerful forces of socialization as in her statement that "women's mothering

does not exist in isolation. It is a fundamental constituting feature of the sexual division of labor. As part of the sexual division of labor, it is structurally and causally related to other institutional arrangements and to ideological formulations which justify the sexual division of labor" (32). Also note her observation that "legitimating ideologies themselves, as well as institutions like schools, the media, and families which perpetuate ideologies, contribute to social reproduction. They create expectations in people about what is normal and appropriate and how they should act" (35).

Nonetheless, Chodorow finds socialization processes inadequate to explain women's nurturant and relational orientations and subordinates these to what she argues is the more powerful, more formative influence of psychodynamic processes within the family.

5. Obviously race and class must also be recognized as classifications that are defined and assigned value within hierarchical cultural systems. See Scott (1986, esp. 1054–1056).

6. Kreps actually lists five characteristics. My analysis eliminates two of these, honesty and caring. The former remains somewhat underdeveloped in his analysis and it is not entirely clear that Kreps, in fact, intends honesty (as contrasted with, for instance, the appearance of honesty or honesty as it might be qualified by compassion and tact) since that could presumably conflict with other named qualities such as nonjudgmental acceptance and trust. I do not deal with the feature of caring, because Kreps discusses it as a global quality that subsumes the other four; it would also be circular to define caring by the quality of caring.

7. My brief allusion here does not do justice to Keller's insightful work. I have not presented it in depth here since that is not necessary for the issue I am discussing, which is that there are alternative ways to conceive autonomy other than as defined in Western culture. In her penetrating analysis Keller offers an incisive and very broad critique of static autonomy as evident in both the production of "knowledge" and, more generally, social practice. Her proposal of dynamic autonomy as an alternative way to conduct science and to live a life is similarly provocative.

7. At a Cultural Crossroad: The Future of Care in the United States

1. An interesting demonstration of the disparity between public acceptance of women's presence in formerly male occupations and lack of public acceptance of any change in women's or men's traditional roles appeared in a 1991 Gallup poll reported in *Newsweek*. This interview

questioned men and women about their opinions of women's involvement in combat duty. While only 21 percent thought women should not be allowed in combat roles, a whopping 89 percent expressed concern about mothers leaving small children at home (plus or minus 5 percentage points margin of error). This suggests that the public generally countenances women's participation in nontraditional roles *only if* they aren't neglecting traditional ones. Since presumably many mothers would have husbands, the poll also suggests people do not generally assume fathers could care adequately for young children while mothers are engaged in war.

2. Whether institutions can actually provide "care" as opposed to, say, attention and medical assistance is currently a matter of dispute. A key axis of this debate involves the tension between an economic model's emphasis on exchange (that is, money for time and attention) and the consensual understanding as caring for others as a kind of giving not contingent on rewards. While it is beyond the scope of my project to pursue this, assessing the compatibility of caring—however defined—with institutional arrangements is an issue that needs to be addressed in a holistic reevaluation of the meaning of care in contemporary Western culture. See Tronto (1989).

3. One of the more convincing challenges to Gilligan's claim that caring is a moral position or ethic is that caring, as construed by Gilligan and as generally understood, is *too* particularistic. Tronto (1987, 1989) and Kerber (1986), among others, have argued that if caring involves only those who are intimates, then there is little to recommend it as an ethic. This view of partiality allows individuals and society to remain unresponsive to many who may "deserve" care as much as those who are fortunate enough to have relationships with individuals who will give it. People who are homeless or ill and without funds or family, for example, would presumably not be cared for given a view of caring as arising exclusively out of personal relationships. Without pushing this position to a universalistic principle it is possible to ask whether we *should* care about those outside of our immediate sphere with whom we have histories and ties that can perhaps too easily account for caring as a personal and vested interest rather than an ethical value. Further, such a restricted view of caring clearly privileges existing relationships and, thus, entails a conservative thrust.

4. Another argument raised against retaining caring's location in the private sphere is that this reinforces traditional gender divisions and, thus, the likelihood that caring will continue to be regarded as something women, but not men, are expected to provide to others. This critique should also be considered in light of Gilligan's implied advocacy that women should embrace the "ethic of caring" and continue

to enact it, regardless of whether the culture as a whole values caring. In arguing this position Gilligan decontextualizing care, removing it from its embeddedness in certain historical, social, and political contexts that necessarily shape its meaning and, importantly, its consequences for women's status in the culture. See Kaplan (1982).

5. It is beyond the scope of this project to elaborate particular strategies for articulating enlarged and public views of caring. Clearly I am calling for political activism in a variety of forms including, but not restricted to, lobbying, voting, assessing candidates on their willingness to include care concerns in legislative agenda, initiatives and coalitions in institutions, letters to the editor of newspapers and popular magazines, and inclusion of care talk within normal social discourse. Elaboration of these and additional strategies for fomenting change is a subject that should command the attention of substantial future work both in and beyond academe.

6. It should be noted that a number of corporations and businesses have not waited for government incentives or worker demands to reform themselves into "family friendly" workplaces. Travelers, for example, innovated support programs for elder care for its employees. In 1990, Stride Rite opened an intergenerational on-site day-care center for children and parents of its employees. A number of other corporations and workplaces have developed various kinds of programs that support families, and most report these not only please employees, but they are financially profitable. See Beck et al., 1990 and Hewlett (1986, 1991).

7. Presenting only this portion of Chodorow's claim is technically a misrepresentation, but I believe it is consistent with the intent of her analysis. In context, Chodorow (1990) also cautions that the relational self "threatens to undermine autonomy and to dissolve the self into others" (121). This important caveat, however, is issued within a discussion of socially construed gender roles which link feeling related to others and specifically caring for others with femininity. If caring were freed of these historical gender associations and socialized into males and females alike the danger Chodorow rightly underlines would be greatly alleviated. Further, if fathers were more involved with children, as my analysis suggests could be the case in a culture that values caring, this would necessarily reduce the intensity of the bond between mothers as daughters that Chodorow (1978) earlier cautioned "may shade too much into connection and not enough separateness" (211).

References

Alcoff, L. (1988). Cultural feminism versus post-structuralism: The identity crisis in feminist theory. *Signs, 13*, 405–436.

Anderson, J. (1991). *Bankrupting America's cities*. Lansing, MI: Employment Research Associates.

Angel, M. D. (1987). *The orphaned adult: Confronting the death of a parent*. New York: Human Sciences Press.

Apter, T. (1990). *Altered loves: Mothers and daughters during adolescence*. New York: St. Martin's.

Aronson, J. (1992). Women's sense of responsibility for the care of old people: "But who else is going to do it?" *Gender and Society, 6*, 8–29.

Barrett, M. (1980). *Women's oppression today: Problems in Marxist feminist analysis*. London: New Left Books.

Barron, R. D., & Norris, G. M. (1976). Sexual divisions and the dual labour market. In D. L. Barker & S. Allen (Eds.), *Dependence and exploitation in work and marriage* (pp. 47–69). London: Longman.

Beck, M., Kantrowitz, B., Beachy, L., Hager, M., Gordon, G., Roberts, E., & Hammill. (1990, July 16). The daughter track. *Newsweek*, pp. 45–54.

Belenky, M. F., Clinchy, B. M., Goldberger, N. R., & Tarule, J. M. (1986). *Women's ways of knowing: The development of self, voice and mind*. New York: Basic Books.

Benhabib, S. (1987). The generalized and the concrete other: The Kohlberg-Gilligan controversy and feminist theory. In S. Benhabib & D. Cornell (Eds.), *Feminism as critique: On the politics of gender* (pp. 77–95). Minneapolis: University of Minnesota Press.

Berg, B. J. (1986). *The crisis of the working mother: Resolving the conflict between family and work*. New York: Summit.

Bettelheim, B. (1943). Individual and mass behavior in extreme situations. *Journal of Abnormal and Social Psychology, 38*, 417–452.

Bleier, R. (1986). *Feminist approaches to science*. New York: Pergamon Press.

Blum, L., Homiak, M., Housman, J., & Scheman, N. (1976). Altruism and women's oppression. In C. C. Gould & M. W. Wartofsky (Eds.), *Women and Philosophy: Toward a theory of liberation* (pp. 222–247). New York: G. P. Putnam.

Blum, L. A. (1988). Gilligan and Kohlberg: Implications for moral theory. *Ethics, 98*, 472–491.

Bordo, S. (1987). *The flight to objectivity: Essays on Cartesianism and culture*. Albany: State University of New York Press.

Brody, E. M. (1985). Parent care as a normative stress. *The Gerontologist,* *25,* 19–29.

Brody, R. (1989–1990). Special report on family. *Whittle Communications.* Knoxville, TN: Whittle Communications.

Broughton, J. M. (1983). Women's rationality and men's virtues: A critique of gender dualism in Gilligan's theory of moral development. *Social Research, 50,* 597–642.

Broverman, I., Broverman, D., Clarkson, F., Rosenkrantz, P., & Vogel, S. (1970). Sex-role stereotypes and clinical judgments of mental health. *Journal of Consulting and Clinical Psychology, 34,* 1–7.

Burleson, B. R. (1984). Comforting communication. In H. E. Sypher & J. L. Applegate (Eds.), *Communication by children and adults: Social cognitive and strategic processes* (pp. 63–104). Beverly Hills: Sage.

Butler, J. P. (1990). *Gender trouble: Feminism and the subversion of identity.* New York: Routledge.

Campbell, K. K. (1973). The rhetoric of women's liberation: An oxymoron. *Quarterly Journal of Speech, 59,* 74–86.

Campbell, K. K. (1983). Femininity and feminism: To be or not to be a woman. *Communication Quarterly, 31,* 101–108.

Chan, V., & Momparler, M. (1991, May/June). George Bush's report card: What's he got against kids? *Mother Jones,* pp. 44–45.

Chodorow, N. J. (1974). Family structure and feminine personality. In M. Z. Rosaldo & L. Lamphere (Eds.), *Woman, culture, and society* (pp. 43–66). Stanford, CA: Stanford University Press.

Chodorow, N. J. (1978). *The reproduction of mothering: Psychoanalysis and the sociology of gender.* Berkeley: University of California Press.

Chodorow, N. J. (1990). What is the relation between psychoanalytic feminism and the psychoanalytic psychology of women? In D. L. Rhode (Ed.), *Theoretical perspectives on sexual difference* (pp. 114–130). New Haven, CT: Yale University Press.

Cirksena, K. (1987). Politics and difference: Radical feminist epistemological premises for communication studies. *Journal of Communication Inquiry, 11,* 19–28.

Cohen, J. (1991). About women and rights. *Dissent,* 371–376.

Coles, R. (1977). *Eskimos, Chicanos, Indians.* Boston, MA: Little, Brown and Company.

Cornell, D. (1991). Sex discrimination law and equivalent rights. *Dissent,* 400–405.

Coughlan, R. (1956, December 24). Changing roles in modern marriage: Psychiatrists find in them a clue to alarming divorce rate. *Life,* pp. 108–112.

de Lauretis, T. (1984). *Alice doesn't: Feminism, semiotics, cinema.* Bloomington: Indiana University Press.

Derrida, J. (1973). *Speech and phenomena, and other essays on Husserl's theory of signs.* Evanston, IL: Northwestern University Press.

de Saussure, F. (1974). *Course in general linguistics.* London: Fontana.

Diamond, I., & Hartsock, N. (1981). Beyond interests in politics: A comment on Virginia Sapiro's "When are interests interesting? The problem of political representation of women." *American Political Science Review, 75,* 717–721.

Dinnerstein, D. (1976). *The mermaid and the minotaur: Sexual arrangements and human malaise.* New York: Harper & Row.

Diwakar, R. R. (1948). *Satyagraha: The power of truth.* Hinsdale, IL: Henry Regnery.

Dubois, E. (1980). Politics and culture in women's history. *Feminist Studies, 6,* 28–36.

Dupré, J. (1990). Global versus local perspectives on sexual difference. In D. L. Rhode (Ed.), *Theoretical perspectives on sexual difference* (pp. 47–62). New Haven, CT: Yale University Press.

Edleman, M. W. (1991, May/June). Kids first. *Mother Jones,* pp. 76–77.

Eichenbaum, L., & Orbach, S. (1983a). *Understanding women: A feminist psychoanalytic approach.* New York: Basic Books.

Eichenbaum, L., & Orbach, S. (1983b). *What do women want: Exploring the myth of dependency.* New York: Coward-McCann.

Eichenbaum, L., & Orbach, S. (1987). *Between women: Love, envy and competition in women's friendships.* New York: Viking.

Eisenstein, H., & Jardine, A. (Eds.) (1980). *The future of difference.* Boston, MA: G. K. Hall.

Eisenstein, Z. (1983). The state, the patriarchal family, and working mothers. In I. Diamond (Ed.), *Families, politics, and public policy: A feminist dialogue on women and the state* (pp. 41–58). New York: Longman.

Eisler, D. (1987). *The chalice and the blade: Our history, our future.* New York: Harper and Row.

Engels, F. (1967). *The origin of the family, private property, and the state.* New York: International Publications. (Original work published 1884)

Faludi, S. (1991). *Backlash: The undeclared war against American women.* New York: Crown.

Ferguson, K. E. (1988). Subject centeredness in feminist discourse. In K. B. Jones & A. G. Jonasdottir (Eds.), *The political interests of gender: Developing theory and research with a feminist face* (pp. 66–78). London, UK: Sage.

Finch, J., & Groves, D. (Eds.). (1983). *A labour of love: Women, work and caring.* London: Routledge and Kegan Paul.

Flax, J. (1978). The conflict between nurturance and autonomy in mother-daughter relationships and within feminism. *Feminist Studies, 4,* 171–189.

Flax, J. (1987). Postmodernism and gender relations in feminist theory. *Signs, 12*, 621–643.

Flax, J. (1990). *Thinking fragments: Psychoanalysis, feminism, and postmodernism in the contemporary west.* Berkeley: University of California Press.

Forum. (1988). *Women's Studies in Communication, 11*, 4–36.

Forum: On *In a Different Voice* [Special issue] (1986). *Signs, 11*.

Foucault, M. (1973). *The birth of the clinic: An archeology of medical perception.* London: Tavistock.

Foucault, M. (1979). What is an author? *Screen, 20*, 13–33.

Freud, S. (1946). *The ego mechanisms of defense.* New York: International University Press.

Friedan, B. (1981). *The second stage.* New York: Summit.

Geertz, C. (1973). *The interpretation of cultures.* New York: Basic Books.

Gilligan, C. (1982). *In a different voice: Psychological theory and women's development.* Cambridge, MA: Harvard University Press.

Gilligan, C. (1986). Reply. Forum: On *In a Different Voice* [Special issue]. *Signs, 11*, 324–333.

Gilligan, C. (1987). Moral orientation and moral development. In E. F. Kittay & D. T. Meyers (Eds.), *Women and moral theory* (pp. 19–33). Totowa, NJ: Rowman & Littlefield.

Gilman, C. P. (1966). *Women and economics: A study of the econo mic relation between men and women as a factor in social evolution.* New York: Harper and Row. (Original work published 1899)

Goodman, E. (1991, July 26). Judge Thomas latest self-made star. *Raleigh News and Observer*, p. 13-A.

Goodman, E. (1992, April 11). Lost dads leave endless longing in children. *Raleigh News and Observer*, p. 15-A.

Graedon, J. (1991, April 6). *The people's pharmacy.* Broadcast by UNC-TV, Chapel Hill, NC.

Grant, J. (1987). I feel therefore I am: A critique of female experience as the basis for a feminist epistemology. *Women and Politics, 7*, 99–114.

Greeno, C. G., & Maccoby, E. E. (1986). How different is the "different voice?" *Signs, 11*, 310–316.

Gwaltney, J. L. (Ed.) (1980). *Drylongso: A self-portrait of black America.* New York: Random House.

Halpern, J. (1987). *Helping your aging parents: A practical guide for adult children.* New York: Macmillan.

Harding, S. G. (1986). *The science question in feminism.* Ithaca, NY: Cornell University Press.

Harding, S. G. (1991). *Whose science? whose knowledge? Thinking from women's lives.* Ithaca, NY: Cornell University Press.

Hare-Mustin, R. T., & Marecek, J. (1990). Gender and the meaning of difference. In R. T. Hare-Mustin & J. Marecek (Eds.), *Making a difference: Psychology and the construction of gender* (pp. 22–64). New Haven, CT: Yale University Press.

Hartsock, N. C. M. (1983). *Money, sex, and power: Toward a feminist historical materialism.* New York: Longman.

Hegel, G. W. F. (1952). *The philosophy of right* (T. M. Knox, Trans.). Clarendon, UK: Oxford University Press.

Helmich, D. L. (1974, Winter). Male and female presidents: Some implications of leadership style. *Human Resource Management* (pp. 25–26).

Henley, N. (1977). *Body politics: Power, sex, and nonverbal communication.* Englewood Cliffs, NJ: Prentice-Hall/Spectrum.

Hewlett, S. A. (1986). *A lesser life: The myth of female liberation in America.* New York: Morrow.

Hewlett, S. A. (1991). *When the bough breaks: The cost of neglecting our children.* New York: Basic Books.

Hochschild, A., with Machung, A. (1989). *The second shift: Working parents and the revolution at home.* New York: Viking-Penguin Press.

Horner, M. S. (1971). Femininity and successful achievement: A basic inconsistency. In M. H. Garskof (Ed.), *Roles women play: Readings toward women's liberation* (pp. 97–122). Belmont, CA: Brooks/Cole.

Houston, B. (1985). *Prolegomena to future caring.* Paper presented at the annual meeting of the Association for Moral Education, Toronto, Canada.

Hull, G. T., Scott, P. B., & Smith, B. (Eds.). (1982). *All the women are white, all the blacks are men, but some of us are brave: Black women's studies.* Old Westbury, NY: The Feminist Press.

Irigaray, L. (1985). *Speculum of the other woman.* Ithaca, NY: Cornell University Press.

Jackson, G. G. (1982). Black psychology: An avenue to the study of Afro-Americans. *Journal of Black Studies, 12,* 241–260.

Janeway, E. (1971). *Man's world, woman's place: A study in social mythology.* New York: Delta.

Jennings, W. S., Kilkenny, R., & Kohlberg, L. (1983). Moral development theory and practice for youthful and adult offenders. In W. S. Laufer & J. M. Day (Eds.), *Personality theory, moral development and criminal behavior* (pp. 281–355). Lexington, MA: Lexington Books.

Jonasdottir, A. (1988). On the concept of interest, women's interests, and the limitations of interest theory. In K. B. Jones & A. G. Jonasdottir (Eds.), *The political interests of gender: Developing theory and research with a feminist face* (pp. 33–65). London: Sage.

Jones, K. B. (1988). Towards the revision of politics. In K. B. Jones & A. G. Jonasdottir (Eds.), *The political interests of gender: Developing theory and research with a feminist face* (pp. 11–32). London: Sage.

Jones, K. B., & Jonasdottir, A. G. (Eds.). (1988). Introduction: Gender as an analytic category in political theory. *The political interests of gender: Developing theory and research with a feminist face* (pp. 1–10). London, UK: Sage.

Kalish, R. A. (1969). The effects of death upon the family. In L. Pearson (Ed.), *Death and dying: Current issues in the treatment of the dying person* (pp. 79–107). Cleveland, OH: Press of Case Western Reserve University.

Kant, I. (1965). *The metaphysical elements of justice* (J. Ladd., Trans.). New York: Liberal Arts Press.

Kanter, R. M. (1977). *Men and women of the corporation.* New York: Basic Books.

Kaplan, T. (1982). Female consciousness and collective action: The case of Barcelona, 1910–1918. In N. O. Keohane, M. Z. Rosaldo, & B. Gelpi (Eds.), *Feminist theory: A critique of ideology* (pp. 55–76). Chicago: University of Chicago Press.

Keller, E. F. (1985). *Reflections on gender and science.* New Haven, CT: Yale University Press.

Keniston, K. (1965). *The uncommitted: Alienated youth in American society.* New York: Harcourt, Brace and World.

Kerber, L. K. (1986). Some cautionary words for historians. *Signs, 11,* 304–310.

Kirkegaard, S. (1957). *The concept of dread* (W. Lowrie, Trans.). Princeton, NJ: Princeton University Press.

Kittay, E. F., & Meyers, D. T. (Eds.). (1987). *Women and moral theory.* New Jersey: Rowman & Littlefield.

Kohlberg, L. (1958). *The development of modes of moral thinking and choice in the years 10 to 16.* Unpublished doctoral dissertation, University of Chicago, Chicago, IL.

Kohlberg, L. (1984). *Essays on moral development* (2 vols.). San Francisco: Harper and Row.

Kreps, G. L. (1990). The nature of therapeutic communication. In G. Gumpert & S. L. Fish (Eds.), *Talking to strangers: Mediated therapeutic communication* (pp. 29–38). Norwood, NJ: Ablex.

Kristeva, J. (1974). La femme, ce n'est jamais ca. *Tel Quel, 57–59,* 19–25.

Kristeva, J. (1981). Women's time. *Signs, 7,* 13–35.

Kristeva, J. (1982). Woman's time. In N. O. Keshane, M. Z. Rosado, & B. C. Gelpi (Eds.), *Feminist theory: A critique of Ideology* (A. Jardine & H. Blake, Trans.) (pp. 31–53). Chicago: University of Chicago Press.

Lacan, J. (1977). *Ecrits.* London: Tavistock.

Leff, M. C. (1980). Interpretation and the art of the rhetorical critic. *Western Journal of Speech Communication, 44,* 337–349.

Luria, Z. (1986). A methodological critique. *Signs, 11,* 316–321.

Mann, J. (1989, March 15). The demeaning "mommy track": Separate but unequal. *Washington Post,* p. C-3.

Markus, M. (1987). Women, success and civil society. In S. Benhabib & D. Cornell (Eds.), *Feminism as critique: On the politics of gender* (pp. 96–109). Minneapolis: University of Minnesota Press.

Mead, G. H. (1934). *Mind, self, and society.* Chicago, IL: University of Chicago Press.

Meese, E. A. (1986). Crossing the double-cross: The concept of difference and feminist literary criticism. In *Crossing the double cross: The practice of feminist criticism* (pp. 69–87). Chapel Hill: The University of North Carolina Press.

Miller, A. (1981). *The drama of the gifted child.* New York: Basic Books.

Miller, J. B. (1976). *Toward a new psychology of women.* Boston, MA: Beacon Press.

Miller, J. B. (1986). *Toward a new psychology of women* (2nd ed.). Boston, MA: Beacon Press.

Mitchell, J. (1975). *Psychoanalysis and feminism: Freud, Reich, Laing, and women.* New York: Vintage Books.

Moi, T. (Ed.). (1986). *The Kristeva Reader.* Oxford: Basil Blackwell.

Moynihan, D. P. (1986). *Family and nation.* San Diego, CA: Harcourt, Brace & Jovanovich.

Nails, D. (1983). Social-scientific sexism: Gilligan's mismeasure of man. *Social Research, 50,* 643–664.

Newsweek (1991, August 5). War and the second sex, pp. 24–29.

Nhat Hanh, T. (1988). *The sun my heart: From mindfulness to insight contemplation.* Berkeley, CA: Parallax Press.

Nobles, W. W. (1976). Extended self: Rethinking the so-called Negro self-concept. *Journal of Black Psychology, 2,* 15–24.

Noddings, N. (1984). *Caring: A feminine approach to ethics and moral education.* Berkeley: University of California Press.

Noddings, N. (1990). Ethics from the standpoint of women. In D. L. Rhode (Ed.), *Theoretical perspectives on sexual difference* (pp. 160–173). New Haven, CT: Yale University Press.

Okin, S. M. (1989). *Justice, gender, and the family.* New York: Basic Books.

Parsons, T. (1953). The superego and the theory of social systems. In T. Parsons, R. F. Bales, & E. A. Shils (Eds.), *Working papers in the theory of action* (pp. 13–29). New York: The Free Press.

Parsons, T. (1964). Age and sex in the social structure of the United States. In *Essays in Sociological Theory* (Rev. ed.) (pp. 89–103). New York: The Free Press. (Original work published 1949)

Penelope (Stanley), J., & Wolfe, S. J. (1983). Consciousness as style: Style as aesthetic. In B. Thorne, C. Kramarae, & N. Henley (Eds.), *Language, gender and society* (pp. 125–139). Rowley, MA: Newbury House.

Petchesky, R. P. (1984). *Abortion and woman's choice: The state sexuality, and reproductive freedom.* New York: Longman.

Polatnick, M. (1973). Why men don't rear children: A power analysis. *Berkeley Journal of Sociology, 18*, 45–86.

Pollak, S., & Gilligan, C. (1982). Images of violence in thematic apperception test stories. *Journal of Personality and Social Psychology, 42*, 159–167.

Poster, M. (1989). *Critical theory and poststructuralism: In search of a context.* Ithaca, NY: Cornell University Press.

Powell, G. N., & Butterfield, D. A. (1981). A note on sex-role identity effects on managerial aspirations. *Journal of Occupational Psychology, 54*, 299–301.

Puka, B. (1990). The liberation of caring: A different voice for Gilligan's "different voice." *Hypatia, 5*, 59–82.

Rakow, L. F. (1989). Feminist studies: The next stage. *Critical Studies in Mass Communication, 6*, 209–215.

Rawls, J. (1971). *A theory of justice.* Cambridge, MA: Harvard University Press.

Rhode, D. L. (1990a). Theoretical perspectives on sexual difference. In D. L. Rhode (Ed.), *Theoretical perspectives on sexual difference* (pp. 1–9). New Haven, CT: Yale University Press.

Rhode, D. L. (1990b). Definitions of difference. In D. L. Rhode (Ed.), *Theoretical perspectives on sexual difference* (pp. 197–212). New Haven, CT: Yale University Press.

Riley, D. (1988). *Am I that name? Feminism and the category of "women" in history.* Minneapolis: University of Minnesota Press.

Robinson, J. P. (1988, December). Who's doing the housework? *American Demographics*, pp. 24–28, 63.

Rodriguez, C. (1990, March/April). Helping Martha Isabel: Did we make a difference? *Utne Reader*, pp. 120–122.

Rosenblum, K. E. (1989). The conflict between and within genders: An appraisal of contemporary American femininity and masculinity. In A. S. Skolnick & J. H. Skolnick (Eds.), *Family in transition: Rethinking marriage, sexuality, childrearing, and family organization* (6th ed.) (pp. 193–202). Glenview, Illinois: Scott-Foresman.

Rowbotham, S. (1973). *Woman's consciousness, man's world.* Harmondsworth, England: Penguin.

Rubin, D. (1982). *Caring: A daughter's story.* New York: Holt, Rinehart and Winston.

Rubin, L. B. (1985). *Just friends: The role of friendships in our lives.* New York: Harper and Row.

Ruble, T. L. (1983). Sex stereotypes: Issues of change in the 1970s. *Sex Roles, 9*, 397–402.

Ruddick, S. (1980). Maternal thinking. *Feminist Studies, 6*, 342–367.

Ruddick, S. (1989). *Maternal thinking: Toward a politics of peace.* Boston, MA: Beacon.

Russo, N. F. (1981). Overview: Sex roles, fertility and the motherhood mandate. In S. Cox (Ed.), *Female psychology: The emerging self* (2nd ed.) (pp. 275–282). New York: St. Martin's.

Sanford, N. (1955). The dynamics of identification. *Psychological Review, 62*, 106–118.

Sapiro, V. (1981). When are interests interesting? the problems of political representation of women. *American Political Science Review, 75*, 701–716.

Schein, V. E. (1975). Relationships between sex role stereotypes and requisite management characteristics among female managers. *Journal of Applied Psychology, 60*, 340–344.

Schwartz, F. N. (1989, January/February). Management women and the new facts of life. *Harvard Business Review*, pp. 65–76.

Schweickart, P. P. (1990). Reading, teaching, and the ethic of care. In S. Gabriel & I. Smithson (Eds.), *Gender in the classroom: Power and pedagogy* (pp. 78–95). Urbana, IL: University of Illinois Press.

Scott, J. W. (1986). Gender: A useful category of historical analysis. *American Historical Review, 91*, 1053–1075.

Sher, G. (1987). Other voices, other rooms? Women's psychology and moral theory. In E. F. Kittay & D. T. Meyers (Eds.), *Women and moral theory* (pp. 178–189). Totowa, NJ: Rowman & Littlefield.

Shulman, A. K. (Ed.). (1972). *Red Emma speaks: Selected writings and speeches*. New York: Random House.

Silverstone, B., & Hyman, H. (1989). *You and your aging parent: The modern family's guide to emotional, physical, and financial problems* (3rd ed.). New York: Pantheon.

Smith, D. E. (1985). Review of Deborah Gorham, *The Victorian girl and the feminine ideal. Labor/Le Travail, 15*, 246–249.

Snitow, A. (1990, March/April). Perestroika in the USA: Bring the gender wall down. *Utne Reader*, p. 84.

Sommers, T., & Shields, L. (1987). *Women take care: The consequences of caregiving in today's society*. Gainesville, FL: Triad Publishing.

Stacey, J. (1983). The new conservative feminism. *Feminist Studies, 9*, 559–583.

Stack, C. (1986). The culture of gender: Women and men of color. *Signs, 11*, 321–324.

Stanback, M. H. (1988). What makes scholarship about black women and communication feminist communication scholarship? *Women's Studies in Communication, 11*, 28–31.

Stanton, E. C., Anthony, S. B., & Gage, M. J. (Eds.). (1881–1886). *The History of Woman's Suffrage* (Vols. 1–3). Rochester, NY: Charles Mann.

Stoller, E. P. (1983). Parental caregiving by adult children. *Journal of Marriage and the Family, 45*, 851–858.

Stoller, R. J. (1964). A contribution to the study of gender identity. *International Journal of Psycho-Analysis, 45*, 220–226.

Tavris, C. (1992). *The mismeasure of woman*. New York: Simon and Schuster.

Tronto, J. C. (1987). Beyond gender difference to a theory of care. *Signs, 12*, 644–663.

Tronto, J. C. (1989). Women and caring: What can feminists learn about morality from caring? In A. M. Jaggar & S. R. Bordo (Eds.), *Gender/body/knowledge: Feminist reconstructions of being and knowing* (pp. 172–187). New Brunswick, NJ: Rutgers University Press.

Unger, R. M. (1975). *Knowledge and politics*. New York: The Free Press.

Van Gelder, L. (1984, January). Carol Gilligan: Leader for a different kind of future. *MS, 12*, 37–40, 101.

Van Leeuwen, M. S. (1990). *Gender and grace: Love, work, and parenting in a changing world*. Downers Grove, IL: Intervarsity Press.

Warren, C. A. B. (1988). *Gender issues in field research*. Newbury Park, CA: Sage.

Weedon, C. (1987). *Feminist practice and poststructuralist theory*. New York: Basil Blackwell.

Welter, B. (1966). The cult of true womanhood: 1820–1860. *American Quarterly, 18*, 151–174.

Winkler, K. J. (1988, September 28). Women's studies after two decades: Debates over politics, new directions for research. *Chronicle of Higher Education*, pp. A4–A7.

Wood, J. T. (1986a). Different voices in relationship crises: An extension of Gilligan's theory. *American Behavioral Scientist*, 273–301.

Wood, J. T. (1986b). Maintaining dual-career bonds: A note on communication and relational structure. *Southern Journal of Speech Communication, 51*, 267–273.

Wood, J. T. (1992a). *Spinning the symbolic web: Human communication and symbolic interaction*. Norwood, NJ: Ablex.

Wood, J. T. (1992b). Telling our stories: Narratives as a basis for theorizing sexual harassment. *Journal of Applied Communication Research, 20*, 349–362.

Wood, J. T. (1993). Enlarging conceptual boundaries: A critique of research in interpersonal communication. In S. P. Bowen & N. J. Wyatt (Eds.), *Transforming Visions: Feminist Critiques of Speech Communication* (pp. 19–49). Cresskill, NJ: Hampton.

Wood, J. T., & Conrad, C. R. (1983). Paradox in the experiences of professional women. *Western Journal of Speech Communication, 47*, 305–322.

Young, I. M. (1985). Humanism, gynocentrism, and feminist politics. *Women's Studies International Forum, 8*, 173–183.

Young, I. M. (1987). Impartiality and the civic public: Some implications of feminist critiques of moral and political theory. In S. Benhabib & D. Cornell (Eds.), *Feminism as critique: On the politics of gender* (pp. 57–76). Minneapolis: University of Minnesota Press.

Name Index

Subject Index

Acceptance of others, 107–8

Business practices: current, 27, 136–37; needed changes, 149–52, 179n.6

Care: defined, 40; for and about, 40; need for, 112, 133–40; transforming views of, 131–61

Caregivers: creation of, 117–18; need for, 20–23; needs of, 174n.4; role of, 18–19

Caregiving: as concrete practice, 106–10; as socially constructed, 41–50, 29–32, 56–60, 87

Caring: as concrete practice, 106–10; as constitutive of woman, 75–76; costs of, 3, 25–26, 50–61; discursively constructed, 29–32, 56–60; generated by power relations, 99–102; inculcating tendencies to, 105–6; need for, 20; personal growth, 27; relation to gender, 5–9, 12–14, 19, 21, 24–27, 33–36, 94–97; situated in culture, 13–14, 87, 92–94, 164–65, 176–77n.4

Caring professions, 24

Child care, 21, 22

Community efforts, 154–55

Compassion trap, 25

Compromised autonomy, 53–56

Costs of caring: compromised autonomy, 53–56; low status, 56–61, 84; motivational displacement, 51–53; strain, 25–26, 163

Costs of not caring, 159–60

Crisis of care, 131–61

Critical posture, 167–69

"Cult of true womanhood," 34–35

Cultural practices, 118–21

Culture: defined, 114; value assigned to caring, 18–19, 24, 26–27, 56–61, 116–22; views of caring, 17–18, 59, 84

Curricular changes, 153

Decontextualized view of care, 13–14, 93–94

Devaluation of caregiving, 18–19, 26–27, 56–61, 84, 114, 115–22

Dichotomizing women and men, 69–71, 166

Discourse: creation of meaning, 16–17, 19–21; cultural ideology, 29–31

Discursive practices, 118–22, 173–74n.1, 179n.5

Discursive sites, 31, 126–28, 147–56

Discursive struggle, 147–56

Discursive turn, 122–30

Dynamic autonomy, 108–10

Educational institutions, changes in, 152–55

Egocentrism, 109–10

Elderly, 22–24

Empathy, 44–47, 91

Employee benefits plans, 151

Essentialism: challenges to, 81–82; debate, 80–85; view of

Julia T. Wood is a professor of speech communication at the University of North Carolina in Chapel Hill, North Carolina, where she teaches and conducts research in close relationships, gender and communication, and feminist science. During her academic career she has authored or coauthored eight books on human communication, group discussion, and interpersonal relationships and edited two others on scholarship in her discipline. In addition, Professor Wood has presented over one hundred papers at professional meetings, contributed chapters to a number of books in her field, and published widely in major journals.

Julia Wood's interest in caring is not entirely academic. She and her husband were personally involved in caring for her father and, later, her mother during the final stages of their lives. Her personal experience, combined with her scholarly background, provide her with a rich foundation for this study of women and care in the United States.